Robert King

HOW TO BLOG FOR PROFIT

HOW TO BLOG FOR PROFIT

A Step by Step Guide for Beginners to Start Blogging from Zero, Writing Great Contents through SEO Optimization and Make Money Generating Passive Income with Online Business

Robert King

The Book is reproduced below with the goal of providing information that is as accurate and reliable as possible. Regardless, purchasing this Book can be seen as consent to the fact that both the publisher and the author of this book are in no way experts on the topics discussed within and that any recommendations or suggestions that are made herein are for entertainment purposes only. Professionals should be consulted as needed prior to undertaking any of the action endorsed herein.

This declaration is deemed fair and valid by both the American Bar Association and the Committee of Publishers Association and is legally binding throughout the United States.

Furthermore, the transmission, duplication or reproduction of any of the following work including specific information will be considered an illegal act irrespective of if it is done electronically or in print. This extends to creating a secondary or tertiary copy of the work or a recorded copy and is only allowed with express written consent from the Publisher. All additional right reserved.

The information in the following pages is broadly considered to be a truthful and accurate account of facts and as such any inattention, use or misuse of the information in question by the reader will render any resulting actions solely under their purview. There are no scenarios in which the publisher or the

Table of Contents

Description...9

Introduction 13

Chapter 1: Types of Blogs 37

Chapter 2: Find A Profitable Niche Market 41

Chapter 3: To Put Your Face on A Blog or Not...............50

Chapter 4: The Difference Between Bloggers and Affiliate Marketers 53

Chapter 5: Starting to Write Blogs................................55

Chapter 6: Basic SEO Tips for Traffic Generation...........61

Chapter 7: Break Down of a Blogger's Income..............70

Chapter 8: Offer Additional High-Quality Content Outside Your Blog 75

Chapter 9: How to Package Your Blog Ideas? 79

Chapter 10: Writing for an Online Audience 91

Chapter 11: How Often Should You Blog?.................. 107

Chapter 12: Forming a Blog Monetization Strategy.... 115

Chapter 13: Mindset in Your Goals.............................*123*

Chapter 14: Common Mistakes in Blogging *131*

Conclusion *140*

Description

The world of blogging is exciting, and it has room for you! Take a leap of faith and grab the opportunity by the horns. You too can be a part of the blogging industry, adding your voice to the greatest in the industry. Once you are comfortable there, you can expand and help individuals reach their fullest potential. No matter your niche, there is room for you to add perspective to the other voices out there. I wish you good luck on your journey, and I hope you achieve the success that you desire.

In this eBook, I have outlined the road to reach the monetization goal, a safe road that will help you reach the desired destination. Just remember that it all depends on your willingness to follow each and every step that I've outlined.

Monetization is most certainly possible. You can make a living out of your online enterprise; your blog. So, start working on the aspects that I've described. I know many of the principles that you have found here might be in direct contradiction with a lot of your preconceived ideas about blogging, but trust me: put my ideas to the test and let me know how they worked.

I'm not saying you should quit your job or stop living and glue yourself to your blog. It could be great for you if you did that, but let me tell you that if you work with dedication, there will eventually come a time when you'll be able to be a full-time blogger and digital producer without having the need for a job elsewhere.

Remember that you need a paid blog hosting; forget about free versions, that's the first step towards commitment. Your blog must be optimized to target your ideal readers, so stick to your segmentation for every strategy and content creation session.

Make sure your blog is well positioned, your content is rich and that you are driving traffic to your blog. The most important thing: acquire your reader's data to create your mailing list and come up with an email marketing strategy. That said, this guide will focus on the following:

- Types of blogs
- Find a profitable niche market
- To put your face on a blog or not
- Have a sense of purpose
- The difference between bloggers and affiliate marketers
- Starting to write blogs
- Basic SEO tips for traffic generation
- Become a professional blogger
- Break down of a blogger's income
- Offer additional high-quality content outside your blog
- How to package your blog ideas
- Using google and social media for profit

- Make constant improvements
- Writing for an online audience
- Common mistakes in blogging... AND MORE!!!

Introduction

Never you understand what a blog is, how to pick your niche, what the blogging industry is looking like, the legalities of blogging, who the industry leaders are, and looking at the trends that are currently being seen or predicted for the future of blogs, you are now ready to get started. Don't feel overwhelmed; this book is going to help you learn exactly what you need and equip you with the tools required to start your own blog.

The Startup Process

There are five steps in the process of starting up a blog. They're brief they are simple, and you can honestly have a blog set up over the course of the weekend. The hardest part about setting up a blog is the actual writing and getting the wording right.

Step One: What Are You Going to Blog About?

This step is an important one because this is where all of the work that you have done in regards to the niche in down is going to come into play. What is your topic? Who is your target audience? What are you trying to accomplish? It's important that you are blogging about something that you are passionate about and that other people are passionate about as well. Be highly specific and narrow down what you are going to focus on with your blog. By doing this, you are ensuring that you have an audience, that you are able to make money, and that your voice will be heard.

Step Two: Domain, Platform, And Web Hosting

For your blog to be online, you need to first look at which platform you are going to use. The most common platform used in word press, but there are other options. But step two is when you are going to pick which platform you're going to use.

Step Three: It's Time to Set Up Your Blog

Step three is when you get to do the fun part. In this step, you are able to choose your name in your domain name, pick your theme, and figure out the look and the feel of your blog. Your domain name should be unique, and it should reflect what your blog is about. It's important when you are choosing your theme that it's also reflecting what your blog is about. Before you make your website live, make sure that you are checking that everything works, that the look is what you want and that it reflects the message you are trying to convey. This is going to be the longest step because as you make decisions, you may realize that other choices have not worked.

Step Four: It's Time to Go Live

After you have tweaked your blog and make sure it's what you want it to look like, then it's time to hit publish. You need to continually make sure that each page on your blog is working, and you need to figure out how you will market your blog as well.

Step Five: It's Time to Write

Great content is what's going to set you apart from your competitors. Make sure that the content that you are writing is valuable to your readers and to others who may be looking for a solution to the problem that you consult.

Tips and Tricks from Other Bloggers:

- Set define goals
- Avoid posts that contain fluff
- Use a blog topic generator tool
- Perform keyword research
- Blog posts should be more than 1500 words
- Make sure to utilize the three types of posts: attention grabbers, how-to, and pillar post
- Break up your content with graphics or videos to keep the readers engaged
- Use block quotes or italics/bold fonts to also break up the content

- When in doubt always add an image or two
- Only use images that are royalty-free or graphics/images where you own the rights
- Utilize tools to create unique images for your social media posts. This allows you to stand out from the competition
- Make sure that you and your posts with a conclusion, question, or a call to action.
- Your headline should be simple but not boring
- Take time to analyze the title of your posts
- Utilize social sharing buttons to allow your readers easier ways to share your content
- At the minimum, post once a week but two times per week is better.
- Use spell checking tools and self-edit your posts.
- Make sure that your post is accurate by fact-checking
- Until you learn the habits of your audience, it is best to post on Monday or Thursday mornings.
- Email any subscribers with your latest posts, but make sure that you are not misusing your email list.
- When you use expert opinions, or you use the advice of other bloggers, it's a good idea to email the post to the individuals you are mentioning.
- Promote your blog post over time

- Make sure that you are responding to any reader engagement
- Revitalize blog content and use it in different ways such as e-books.
- Don't give up
- Submit Your Post to Niche Bookmarking Sites
  - Growth factors
  - Inbound.org
  - Triberr
  - Hacker news
  - Biz sugar

Submit Your Post to Popular Bookmarking Sites

- StumbleUpon
- Dig
- Reddit
- Develop and Using Editorial Calendar for Blog
  - Published date
  - Author
- Keyword
  - Topic/content ideas
  - Headline/title
  - Linked to a working document
  - Link to publish content

- Column for each avenue you will promote this long: social media, networks, email blasts, and or each

- Make a list of content that you feel confident in creating

- Explore the:

  - Pain points of your customer problem to help them solve

  - The answer, questions in your industry

- Explore subjects that you are interested in yourself

- If you have a current website, just simply build the blog into that.

- Invest in blog user experience and design

- Utilize Google Analytics to measure your results

  - Visitors

  - Referrals

  - Bounce rate

  - Exit pages

  - Conversion rates

  - Landing pages

Checklists for An Effective Blog Post

- After publishing

- Creating a second pin

- Share with social media

- Share to groups and communities

- Check search engine optimization again

- Turn it into a new piece of content

- Reply to comments

- Extended with future posts

- Before you publish

- Ensure that your title is catchy

- Make sure it can be read easily

- Search engine optimize your post

- Proofread

- Add optimized images

- Manage your images

- Add alternate text your images

- Ensure that you end with the CTA and a question

- Add links to other posts

- Use the featured image

- Make it available for download

- Make it shareable

- Give credit to your sources

- Hit publish

Picking A Name

Picking a name is sort of fun, but it can be a pain. There are blog name generator tools that are available for free on the Internet, but before you resort to that try to come up with one on your own. Follow the steps below to create a blog that you are going to love, and that will stand the test of time.

There's No Hurry

There may be a need to rush for some people who are trying to get their blog off the ground, but picking a blog name is the most important step other than picking your niche. Consider all of your options when you pick a name and make sure that you have, with the perfect name for you. Changing your blog name down the line is going to require you to change the donor may name, change the social media accounts, and more. Making sure that you take your time is so important because then you are able to ensure that you don't have to make changes on the road.

Attention-Grabbing and Short

It's important to make sure that your domain name or your blog name is short and is going to grab the attention of readers. It's important to make sure that people can find you on the Internet.

Not too Specific

Even if your niche is quite specific, make sure that you are not making your blog name two specific. If your blog name is too specific, you will not be able to expand your blog later down the road. Keep this in mind as you are choosing your name.

Think Twice About Using Your Personal Name

The only time using your personal name in your blog name is if you are the sole owner of a business and even then, it's not a good idea. It is a good idea to use your personal name if you're a writer and you're promoting your writing. Otherwise, try to find a name that is catchy and memorable that is going to work better over the long run.

Skip Special Characters or Numbers

Don't use exclamation points or Asterix, among other special characters in your blog name. Also, skip the numbers. Hyphens are sometimes used to make the name more readable but pass on those as well.

No Brand Names or Trademarks

It's best to avoid using that your domain name. Even portions could be violating copywriting laws.

Name Generators and Thesauruses Are Excellent Tools

There are tools and apps out there that can help you choose a blog name. If you're really stuck, and you can't figure out which way to go, it's a good idea to utilize one of the sources.

Ask Friends

If you're stuck, ask your friends, your coworkers, or even family members what a good name would be. Often times you will be surprised where the best name is going to come from. It's especially valuable to ask these individuals if they are part of your target audience.

How to Use AdSense Effectively

This part of the book will provide you with advanced techniques. These techniques are designed to boost your earnings from Google's AdSense program. By applying these techniques on your site, you can double (or even triple) your income from AdSense.

It's important to point out that each blog is unique. Even blogs that belong to the same niche can have different layouts, readers, and articles. These elements greatly influence potential earnings from the AdSense program. However, the techniques given below can help you with your AdSense campaign regardless of your niche, layout, and current blog entries.

1. Place ads on places that attract the readers' eyes – Keep in mind that you earn money from AdSense each time a reader clicks on the displayed ads. That means you need to place those ads in the attractive parts of your blog. However, you also need to consider the overall usability of your site. If you will place AdSense ads with reckless abandon, readers might stop visiting your blog. To gain maximum benefits from AdSense, you need to master the art of ad placement.

2. Target specific parts of your blog entries – With this technique, you will pinpoint the exact parts of your articles that Google must check when choosing ads. Implementing this

technique on your blog is simple and easy. You just have to type "<!-- google_ad_section_start →" to indicate the place where Google should start checking. Then, use "<!-- google_ad_section_end → to indicate the endpoint for Google's analysis.

3. Use the plugin called "Quick AdSense" - This plugin, which is offered by the WordPress system, lets you incorporate AdSense ads into your articles. With this tool, you can choose different criteria to customize the placements of your ads.

Important Note: According to experienced bloggers, the best spot to place an ad is right under the title of a blog entry. You can use Quick AdSense to place ads on that spot.

4. Blend colors – When the AdSense program was introduced, bloggers used loud colors to make ads more interesting. These days, however, bloggers change the colors of AdSense ads so that they blend with the site's theme. The main disadvantage of the old strategy is that it destroys the overall beauty of the blog. The newer strategy resolves this problem by making sure that the blog and the ads are pleasing to the readers' eyes.

5. Create articles for online searchers – You probably have regular readers and visitors from search engine results. In most cases, bloggers don't exert much effort on meeting the needs of visitors who used search engines.

It is true that most of these visitors won't return to your blog again. You need to embrace this fact if you want to succeed as a blogger. Keep in mind that you created a blog to share helpful articles with other people. Thus, you shouldn't worry about the number of times your readers visit your blog.

Search for the keywords used by online searchers. Then, incorporate those keywords to your articles. It doesn't mean that you will ignore your regular readers. Rather, you will write materials that can satisfy the needs of anyone who will visit your blog.

6. Install the search bar of Google – Google is one of the leading search engines today. Its search capabilities are stronger than that of any blogging platform. By installing Google's search bar on your blog, you can help readers find the information they need and earn some money. The results of the online searches come with standard ads, just like typical search results of the Google engine.

7. Connect AdSense and Google Analytics – By linking AdSense and Google Analytics, you can obtain loads of data about your earnings. This technique will help you determine your most profitable articles and best keywords. It can also pinpoint the third-party websites that send the most volume of traffic to your blog. As an AdSense user, you should take advantage of this option.

How to Pick a Niche

Welcome to part two. In this section, we will discuss the significance of selecting the right specialty for your blog. This is fundamental for your prosperity in such a case that you don't pick the correct specialty, well then lord have mercy on you. On the off chance that you select the wrong specialty for your blog, at that point you should bid a fond farewell to your fantasies of turning into a full-time blogger.

With regards to choosing the correct specialty for your blog, there are numerous interesting points before you pick the correct subject.

Unexpectedly, you don't need a theme which is "super-specialty" implying that it would be difficult for somebody to direct people to the site. In conclusion, it might be ideal on the off chance that you ensured that there are incredible partner alternatives for the specialty. Allowed most specialties have associate choices at the same time, "Are they going to profit?" that is another inquiry to consider.

So, what we will do in this part is demonstrate to you the most searched after systems to discover a specialty explicit to you and your aptitude. In addition, give you a few instruments on the most proficient method to discover a subject to compose on which is as of now getting the perfect measure of traffic for you to begin winning some cash. Right away, how about we get into the fundamentals of this part.

Pick a niche you like

On the off chance that you are not messing around with what you are expounding on, at that point chances are you won't make a dime from it. Individuals are splendid at sniffing out somebody who isn't associated with the point. It is an absolute necessity that whichever specialty you choose to begin your blog on should be something you are keen on or if nothing else remotely intrigued.

The most ideal approach to discover your specialty is ask yourself what your interests are and leisure activities. On the off chance that I adore yoga and do yoga normally, at that point that could be a possibility for you. Ask yourself what your pastimes or interests are. Everyone has an enthusiasm or diversion they appreciate. I am very certain that you do too, so discover it and compose it.

Small scale specialty

When you have settled on a point to compose on, it would be a great opportunity to find out about the challenge. To discover, look through your specialty on Google and search for the "About" directly underneath the web index.

You will see a number which is probably in the millions. You need to take a gander at a number which is under 50 million or more 1 million for it to be in the "sweet spot" for choosing the correct specialty. Anything over 50 million would rise to high immersion, and under 1 million would mean there is a lesser shot of you making it gainful.

Affiliate marketing

In later sections, we will examine partner promoting further. It is pivotal that you do some exploration and discover your chances in your chose specialty before you begin your blog. For perusers that have no clue about what partner promoting is, it is the place you have an item on your blog with a connection just interesting to your site. At whatever point somebody chooses to purchase that particular item from your connection, you will get a commission.

Offshoot advertising is the means by which most, if not all, bloggers acquire their cash, so don't ignore this progression. The most ideal approach to see whether your theme has the correct offshoot program is go to Amazon.com and check every one of the items available to be purchased identified with your specialty. In the event that they have a great deal of items accessible for you to advertise, at that point you have discovered the one. In a later section, we will talk about more alternatives in regards to partner promoting, however for the time being, stress over Amazon and the items they bring to the table.

Monetizing

Monetizing your blog site indicates that you will certainly permit Google to run advertisements on your blog site. Whenever individuals click onto that advertisement, you will certainly earn money. The very best method to learn if your particular niche is obtaining a great deal of Google advertising and marketing, simply google your "search phrase."

If your subject is yoga exercise, Google yoga exercise in the search bar. The even more advertisements you see pertaining to your particular niche, the much better possibilities you have of generating income from monetizing your blog site. Generating income from is an excellent method to make some even more cash from your blog site, specifically if you have several site visitors to your blog site.

Final research

Currently to secure the handle your subject, you require to go onto "Google patterns." This is where you will certainly discover exactly how constant your subject is and also the number of individuals are proactively trying to find posts on your particular niche. All you need to do is key in your search phrase right into the internet search engine, as well as it will certainly offer you with a chart.

Ensure you are considering a chart with at the very least 5 years of information. Currently if your representation remains in the center to high mark while remaining constant at the very same time, after that you have actually selected the right subject. Whereas if your chart is gradually decreasing year by year, after that it is time for you to discover a brand-new blog site subject.

If all these standards look into, after that you have the appropriate particular niche and also you can begin your blog site as soon as possible. If that's not the instance, after that I desire you to reassess your subjects and also think of a brand-new one which does satisfy all the requirements detailed above.

Nevertheless, you require to ensure that you are earning money from your blog site as well as not simply composing for it. Maintain browsing as well as maintain looking, as well as you will certainly locate your gold subject. Believe me, you must have the ability to locate your subject within a number of shots.

Benefits of Using WordPress

Creating your blog is essential. There are many Wordpress.com technical guides out there that will support you in creating your blog, but few are really designed to help you optimize your blog from a marketing front. That being said, if your blog is not optimized from a marketing standpoint, you are not going to have the best chances at retaining readers and converting them into customers. You need to consider the marketability of your blog website. In this chapter, we will optimize your blog so that readers are not only captivated by your page the first time they land on it, but they are inspired to follow you, bookmark you, and look for you on other platforms so they can stay up-to-date with all of the great content you share.

Your Template

The first part of having a strong, marketable blog is making sure that you are using the right template. On WordPress, there are hundreds of templates to choose from. If you do not find what you love on their website, you can do a Google search and find many other third-party companies who build WordPress templates that you can install and upload to your blog.

When you are choosing a template, there are a few things that you need to look for. First, you need to make sure that the template actually matches the look of your brand. You do not want to have a minimalist brand using a retro template, or a modern restaurant using a traditional theme. Pay attention to the look and make sure that you can genuinely see your own personal brand matching with it well.

Next, you need to consider functionality. The template you choose should make it easy for readers to locate everything. There should also be a spot where you can easily put a call to action in place that will draw your readers out to your email capturing service and your social media pages. If there is not one built into the template, make sure you can easily envision where one would go and that it would genuinely look as though it fits in and not like it was sloppily tossed in after the fact.

Lastly, you need to choose a template that is mobile ready. Most of your readers will be reading you from their phone. A shrinking number of people visit your site from a desktop, so while you want to make sure that you are desktop compatible as well, keeping your page mobile-friendly is important. Any blogs that are not optimized for mobile devices are quickly skipped over in favor of ones that are. Do not forget to check what the template looks like on mobile and make sure that all of the features are still functional, easy to see, and easy to read so that your reader can enjoy your blog.

Incorporating Your Brand

As you optimize your WordPress blog, make sure that you are incorporating your brand into it. In the "Personalization" tab you can find many different customizations you can make. Specific customizations that are available will depend based on what theme you have chosen. Double check each of these to make sure that they incorporate your brand color, text, and design. This will keep your page looking uniform and will make sure that people can easily identify you. Take some time to really focus on making sure that your brand integrates in a way that is stunning. Simply throwing your colors on the template is not enough. Consider which highlight and base colors you will use and how they fit into your template to make sure that they look amazing. People are a lot pickier about this these days, so make sure you are catering to their need to be visually enticed so that they are more eager to stick around.

Your branding on your WordPress page is like your storefront. If it looks attractive and enjoyable, people will be more likely to bookmark you and come back. If it looks mediocre, they will take what they need, but they probably will not come back. If it looks any less than that, they will probably find a new page altogether to find the information that they are looking for.

Keeping It Simple

Your website should be easy to understand. Many people like to look at their page as a flowing process. Your new or potential reader should land on your page and know exactly what to do and where to go. Ideally, the first place they should look is your blog. Then, when they become interested in you, they will click over to your about page. There, they should be introduced to all of what you do. So, if you have a store or a brand that actually sells things (courses, handmade products, etc.)

For your call to action that captures their email, you should have this simple as well. Keep it in an easy-to-access spot that exists on all of the main pages so that when your new visitor becomes interested, they can input their email to receive their freebie and get more information about your blog and your brand. Ideally, you should also include a delayed pop up that allows your new visitor to input their email. That way if they forget to do it whilst on the pages they are visiting, they are prompted to do it before they leave. Make sure that the pop up is able to be exited by your visitor in case they do not want to give you their email. Pop-ups that cannot be exited are actually considered spam and can result in your page not ranking. Furthermore, WordPress does not allow them.

Your External Integration Features

Make sure that all of your external integration features are set up properly. The last thing you want is for someone to go to input their email and be drawn to a broken link or taken to a ClickFunnel or AWeber site that is not yours. Double check everything you create to make sure it works properly. Ideally, you should navigate your blog as though you are a visitor and test each feature as such as well. This will ensure that you are keeping your links optimized and that all of the features work properly.

Chapter 1: Types of Blogs

Aside from writing a blog in a particular niche, there are a great myriad of types of blogs one can write. I have listed the categories below, but this list is not a limiting defining factor by any means, as there are many more types of blogs that I could list, and the possibilities of types of blogs that can be created are in reality endless.

Money blogs - Blogs focused on techniques for acquiring wealth, this could be a blog that tries to pick the stock market, or a blog that covers the various areas of running a particular type of business. The consistent theme here is that these blogs all focus on engaging in specified activities that will result in an increase in wealth. Most of the readers of these kinds of blogs have an interest in getting rich.

How does a money blog turn a profit?

A money blog will turn a profit by eventually selling products to the reader that correlate directly with the niche the blog focuses on (the sheer variety of money-making niches is almost endless) and what the articles in the blog talk about. The products the blog tries to sell might be a video course or a book that the owner of the blog created explaining in detail a method for making money, such as a how to make money in the stock market course, or it might be an affiliate product.

Tutorial blogs - These are blogs that show you how to do something, and are educational blogs. Though it may not all be only tutorials, a large percentage of the content that attracts readers to these kinds of blogs are indeed the tutorials. Readers continue to read these types of blogs to learn how to get better at something (the sheer variety of niches that tutorials for things could be written about is also nearly endless).

How does a tutorial blog turn a profit?

A tutorial blog will turn a profit by recommending products that will teach you how to do something in greater detail than the articles in the blog. This product can be a video course or book made by the owner of the blog, or they could be affiliate products.

Travel blogs - These are blogs that focus on travel, where the blogger is a traveler and writes about his/her experiences and adventures in other lands. Travel blogs usually upload lots of photos. They might also write reviews of certain products related to travelling, such as certain pieces of travel gear that served them well.

How does a travel blog turn a profit?

The travel blog will usually make money off of some product the blog sells providing the reader with information that they could not get anywhere else (like a guidebook showing you where to buy the best coconuts at the best price in Chiang Mai). The travel blog might also turn a profit by providing affiliate links for travel products that they review.

Lifestyle blogs - A lifestyle blog could indeed be a travel blog, or a money blog, or another kind of blog, and the line is gray as to what actually constitutes a lifestyle blog. However, a lifestyle blog generally is a blog that talks about and promotes living a particular type of lifestyle in which others are interested in (even if those who read the blog don't really live that kind of lifestyle themselves).

How does a lifestyle blog turn a profit?

As with the other types of blogs, a lifestyle blog turns a profit by trying to sell products related to a certain aspect of the lifestyle the blog is promoting. These products may be created by the owner of the blog, but are usually affiliate products.

Review blogs - A review blog is a blog that reviews products within a particular niche. For example, a review blog might review notebook computers, and cover all the various kinds of notebook computers and have its own rating system for reviewing notebook computers. Each blog post will likely be a review of a new notebook computer that just came out.

How does a review blog turn a profit?

A review blog mostly makes money from the affiliate links provided on each product it reviews. A review blog might also come out with its own product related to the niche in which it reviews products in, but most of the money with a review blog tends to be earned from its affiliate links in its reviews.

There are many other types of blogs, and I'm not going to get into them all, but as we can see from this list, the way most blogs make money is by either selling their own products or promoting affiliate products, which means you need to get good at either one or the other, or both. I tend to engage in both!

Chapter 2: Find A Profitable Niche Market

You probably have some friends with individual personal blogs that are of all their interests - images of their kids and videos reviews and talk about their winning super bowl team, and everything in between.

While this is fine for your own personal blog, if you want to blog more professionally you should filter your focus area.

A blog that has a clear identification is more likely to achieve success than one with a wide focus. An individual personal blog is about you while an experienced blog is about the subject.

You can and should be friendly and discuss your tale, but only as it requires the subject at hand.

Before you begin doing anything else to begin your blog site, you should figure out your subject. Your niche industry will affect the domain name you select, the design of your website, and your ideal publishing routine to attraction to the most visitors close to you.

Research the Market

Picking the right market for a new blog can be challenging. You want to discover a subject that is well-known enough to draw in attention and generate income, but one that hasn't already been oversaturated with bloggers giving their opinions.

Finding a new viewpoint on a subject, something that individuals aren't already composing a blog about, gives you the best possibility of getting it in the business long-term - if it's a place where attention prevails, and the key the purpose, why there are no bloggers on the subject, isn't because no one wants to learn about it.

The only way to know is by exploring the place.

The bigger curiosity about a given subject, small-sized portion of the total business you need to catch to achieve success, and the more specific your niche industry will be to offer a new speech.

Let's use a meals blog as an example. Meals are a subject that passions a wide range of people the overall prospective viewers is massive, but there are an accordingly large number of blogs already discussing meals.

Even if you filter it down - say, to a blog about cooking - you'll already discover thousands of other blogs already doing that.

The curiosity about the place is really a great level you'll need to filter it down again. Maybe you're a vegetarian and want to discuss dishes for creating traditional convenience meals that are vegan-friendly.

You'll probably discover there are quite a few vegetarian bloggers out there, but luxury meals the position could allow you to just different enough to be a new speech in the discussion and there are enough individuals fascinated in the subject that all of you can discuss the listeners and achieve success.

Now let's say you have a less well-known topic - we'll use guitar fix as an example.

Guitar fix is a practical subject that many individuals will want in, from expert artists to band administrators to those who play equipment for fun, but it won't include quite so wide a team as cooking.

You might do a case study to get there are a lot of guitar review blogs, but not as many that concentrate on a fix.

Not only do you not need to break your subject down further into "wind instrument repair" or "on the fly maintenance for rock musicians" but concentrating on more will probably filter your subject too much.

There aren't as many competitors for guitar fix blogs as there is for meals blogs, but the number of fascinated visitors is also more compact, the significance you need to draw in a bigger portion of fascinated visitors to achieve success.

Another way to think about this is to have a concentrate on viewer's size in mind numerically. Let's say you want to achieve 1,000 exclusive subscribers members.

On the surface, greater viewers seem to offer you with the best mathematical possibility of being able to discover more visitors.

If there are 100,000 individuals fascinated in X and only 10,000 fascinated in Y that might seem to offer you with 10 times as many opportunities to fantastic an innovative audience.

But if 1,000 everyone is already composing a blog about X and only ten are composing a blog about Y that means the small-sized team will, however, have more available visitors per blogger.

With X, you'd have to fight another blogger to take away some discuss of their viewers if you want to achieve your goal; with Y, you could hypothetically achieve your focus on viewers without having to discuss visitors with any other blogger.

The marketplace may be more compact, but it's also less soaked.

Of course, things hardly ever exercise that easily in reality, but the ultimate factor continues to be.

The best niche for a new blog in 2017 isn't actually the one with the most important following or the one that's the most unique; the best companies are the one that allows you to be a new speech for a group that will be able to support you.

You shouldn't believe what kind of activity prevails on a given blog the subject before you begin doing your pursuit.

Some subjects might seem like they'd be hugely well-known but turn out to be relatively unusual once you've done your pursuit, which makes them perfect prospective niche areas for you.

Conversely, you might think you're the only one fascinated in a given concept idea, only to look for the free blogger from Google already flooded with others writing on your clever industry.

Take notices as you do your pursuit to destroy two parrots with one rock.

Bookmark blogs you like, either because of their look or the way with words of the writer, and then study those for concepts ideas once your site is set up.

If the weblogs are in your industry, sign up for their subscriber list, pay attention to their content, and consider leaving comments and become part of their group once you've got your blog site set up.

It's never too beginning to begin to build a good reputation (and good habits) in your composing a blog career.

Why you?

The blog itself is not the product you're supplying the customer. The site is more like an online store. Items that are up for sale are your thoughts and skills, as communicated through your content.

To entice visitors to your blog site, you need to give them grounds to pay attention to what you, specifically, have to say about a given subject.

Why would someone want to study your blog site instead of the ones already established?

For example, let's use the main subject of expert professional football. There's a huge target on viewers, but what value do you have to offer to readers?

Do you have an inside connection to the players?

A new method of research for the games?

Referring to how much you like something might be fun for you, but it's not very exciting to study.

The best bloggers have either an advanced level of about their subject or bring an innovative viewpoint to the table.

Even if a given industry has large prospective viewers and not many competitive comments, you won't entice any visitors if you don't have anything exciting to say about the subject.

Before you help create your ultimate decision on which concentrate on explore, ask yourself that simple question: why me?

You should be able to offer a one-sentence answer that can create someone fascinated by reading what you have to say.

Logistics

If your blog site fits normally into your routine and lifestyle, it'll be easier for you to put in the effort of keeping it, and you'll be less likely to feel confused or quit due to burn-out.

Ensure that case study, composing, and marketing you'll need to do in your preferred companies are genuine for your life before you settle on a subject.

If you want to create about the local music field, you'll have to try of going to a lot of shows - maybe not the best concept idea if you have to awaken beginning every day for work.

If you want to create a financial blog, you need to be able to keep up with industry styles and provide appropriate advice to your visitors who are keeping track of on you to guide them through quickly changing scenery.

The niche industry you select will also have an effect on how you get to take advantage of your blog site. If you're composing in a bigger industry, your rate of fly-by visitors do it again visitors might be greater.

You'll get a lot of website opinions that would attraction to promoters, but may have a more complicated time promoting affiliate products items.

Conversely, a blog in a small niche industry that has a faithful primary of supporters might not get as much visitors, but the per-visitor benefit could be greater because those visitors buy products items and services, whether they're unique to you or sold by an affiliate.

Chapter 3: To Put Your Face on A Blog or Not

When you're just starting your blog, you have the option to put your face on it, or not put your face on it. What I mean when I say put your face on it doesn't necessarily mean putting a picture of you on your blog, but it means revealing your identity.

If you have a very reputable job, and if your passion is something that could detract from that reputable image, then putting your face on a blog is something that you might not want to do.

Thus, the choice to put your face on a blog or not is entirely personal.

Though I would say that if you can put your face on your blog and get away with it, it's much better. Since when someone puts their face on a blog, readers can feel that they are reading the blog posts of a real person, and thus trust can be built a lot faster. That said, this doesn't mean that you can't earn a profit with a blog that doesn't have your face on it, because you definitely can. Most of my blogs, for example, don't have my face on them, because I don't want others to know that I write them.

So, as a rule of thumb, if your niche is something that you don't want other people knowing you're into, but you're passionate about it, then by all means blog anonymously under some pen name. Though if you can put your face on a blog and would feel no shame whatsoever about it, then by all means do so.

It's truly a personal choice if you want to put your face on your blog or not, and you should also consider the fact that if your blog's traffic were to suddenly skyrocket, do you really want everyone knowing who you are wherever you go?

Many bloggers with their face on their blog get recognized when they go out in public, and sometimes that can be a good thing if people like you, but sometimes it could cause problems if there are a lot of people out there who despise what you stand for.

The reality is that every blog has its share of those who hate everything the blogger stands for, so don't expect everyone to like you. As hard as it is to believe, even I have my fair share of haters, which is exactly why most of my blogs don't have my face on them.

Therefore, please use your best judgement when deciding whether you want people to know who you are or not. And if you do decide to put your face on your blog, then please do not tell people where you live, and if you must provide an address for something, be sure to get a PO Box or some similar-type mailbox that doesn't reveal where you actually reside.

Chapter 4: The Difference Between Bloggers and Affiliate Marketers

While bloggers might not consider themselves affiliate marketers, the reality is that bloggers are definitely affiliate marketers, but just one particular type of affiliate marketer, being the type who writes a blog.

There are many other types of affiliate marketers from Youtubers, to Webmasters, to anyone who posts affiliate links on various non-blog websites. And since this is not an affiliate marketing book, but a book on blogging, I'm not going to get into all the various ways affiliate marketing can be done (it's quite a bit), but instead we'll only focus on how bloggers should be doing affiliate marketing. I would say though, that the moment you post your first affiliate link on your blog, you suddenly become an affiliate marketer. However, you are still a blogger!

Don't change your label and call yourself an affiliate marketer, you should continue to proudly refer to yourself as a blogger! Just because you engage in affiliate marketing doesn't mean you have to call yourself an affiliate marketer, even though the moment you put up that first affiliate link you actually are one. As the art of pure affiliate marketing is not at all about blogging, and someone who blogs while engaging in affiliate marketing is not in the purest sense an affiliate marketer.

I mean if you think about it, to be a blogger you have to wear many types of hats (writer, web designer, reporter, business owner, etc.). So, does it really mean that since you engage in all of those tasks that you suddenly have to accept all of those labels? Well, you do to some extent, but if it's all in the name of blogging, then you're actually a blogger, and all the other hats you wear just kind of go with the territory of blogging.

The lines might blur as to what you really are at times, and it may sometimes seem like you're having an identity crisis, but the good news is that as long as you believe in your heart that you are a blogger, then you will be a blogger! So, keep believing! You are a blogger!

Chapter 5: Starting to Write Blogs

How would I know whether I require a BLOG? What is a Blog in any case? I know what a site is, however what is a blog? A blog is another rendition of a site. It can change every last day and enable guests to communicate with it. How about we backpedal to sites for one moment.

Site = a gathering of one page or progressively that have static content. They take propelled skills to assemble and are mind boggling to refresh and keep up. More often than not the content continues as before upon each visit to it. Individuals visit once to peruse content once in a while to return once more.

Sites are Stagnant Water... in any case

Blog = a current site. It can change every last day with new content. Blogs are extremely straightforward and simple to refresh. There is normally a header and a side bar that stay consistent with the inside content changing with refreshes. Articles composed can be connected back to the principle thought. This conveys traffic to your page. Individuals keep on coming back to perceive what is new. Blogs are jabbering rivulets.

Blogs are dynamic and have quick setup ... sites are static and moderate

How would I know whether I require a blog?

A blog can be utilized by anybody conveying a message. I know you are stating to yourself, I don't have a message to share. My response to you is ~ yes you do, you won't not know it yet but rather stay with me and I will demonstrate to you how you can profit by blogging.

Blogs can help Churches and other non-benefit associations get the message out, blogs can help those of us who offer something (make-up, Jewelry, land, offer on Etsy or eBay), blogs can help organizations who give administrations (PC repair, beauticians, or exterior decorators). Blogs have even helped my child, Nick, improve as an author. I trust a blog ought to be utilized by everybody. Blogs have various regions that assistance Google discover you less demanding. A subset leads back to the ace blog and reveals to Google you are critical. The subsets reinforce the fundamental page.

To answer a couple of questions I have gotten and reacted to about blogging continue perusing.

How would I know a blog will help my congregation? A congregation would utilize a blog this way... Rather than a site (stale water) a congregation would compose on a blog. They would have their header on the best (telling which church they are and perhaps a telephone number and so on) the side could have sermon hours and so on, and the center would contain moving content.

They may examine plans for the future on another blog and connection back to the ace blog, upholding and reinforcing the blog according to Google. Pledge drives could rapidly and effectively be included and shared. Individuals would be slanted to come back to perceive what was new; to feel associated somehow and to feel some portion of the congregation in general.

Blogs get per users returning.

How would I know a blog will help me as a Real Estate Professional?

You offer land. In the past you conveyed post cards telling individuals in the area that you simply sold a house where they live and that you would happily list theirs available to be purchased as well. These shading postcards you mail out are costly to print and mail. Also, you have no assurance they are being conveyed to the person fit for consenting to the deal. They may really get conveyed to a tenant or not land by any means. This is all in or all out publicizing.

Then again, you could set up a blog telling about you as a land proficient in the city you live. This limits the pursuits down in Google when somebody is searching for house purchasing or offering. They can look into this "I need to offer my home in Loxahatchee Florida. You have a more noteworthy shot of being seen marking yourself particularly. Each blog you compose can coordinate back to your lord blog about you. Regardless of what blog they read or offer, they will dependably have your contact data. Another illustration, you may expound on the lodging market in Loxahatchee or you may expound on houses you have available to be purchased that are 3 room and 3,000 sq. feet. One more case could be: a blog about open houses you will be leading in the territory.

Shouldn't something be said about your gems or make-up business ~ by what method can a blog help you? All things considered, the way things are currently you interface with individuals you know and endeavor to get them engaged with hosting a get-together. They welcome their loved ones to go to. You at that point set up an opportunity to meet these individuals, demonstrate to them what you bring to the table (your message) and want to make a deal. This includes conveying items with you to discuss, offer, and show. Consequently, you offer the entertainer something: an unconditional present or credit to use towards items.

Consider this... you set up a blog. This blog encourages you associate with individuals in your general vicinity and abroad. You can expound on specials you are having through particular blogs that interface back to your lord blog. You can indicate pictures or recordings of things and clarify every one. Adornments things appeared on your blog can connect to an online request shape permitting individuals not neighborhood to buy. Individuals in the zone can contact you by means of a frame to set up a gathering as well.

How would I utilize a blog for family correspondence?

Another gathering of individuals who could profit by blogging is a family. I adore scrap-booking and keep collections with my little girl and child as they develop. The main route for it to be seen is for somebody to visit my home. My loved ones not nearby would have no real way to hear or see what is going on with us. A family blog would begin with who is in the family, times of everybody, and some other data important to begin a family bond. The subset (blogs that associate back to the ace blog) could discuss Thanksgiving plays at school, the Mother's Day casual get-together, kindergarten graduation, and some other family occasion you need to impart to the family. Pictures and video would make an incredible expansion to the composed content.

There is a misguided judgment that you must be a master to have a blog. A blog can be overseen by anybody and is an approach to pass on a message. Possibly you have an extraordinary approach to develop orchids or mesh hair. In the event that you have an enthusiasm for it, another person does as well. Offer it. Try not to be hesitant to express your insight and make gigantic move. Your message could be as basic as telling a group you exist and refresh them about happenings to the enormous pledge drive your school or association. It could likewise be an approach to associate with your family and companions and to refresh them about what is going on the home front. In case you have an enthusiasm for something share it with the world through a blog.

Chapter 6: Basic SEO Tips for Traffic Generation

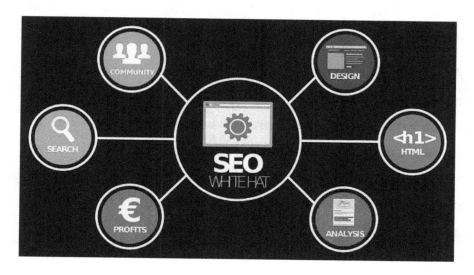

Search engine optimization is a buzzword that has been thrown around the Internet for some time. The reality of the situation is that search engine optimization is necessary if you want to have a successful blog, but the extent that it is necessary is often overestimated. Often, people get a completely incorrect idea of what search engine optimization actually is.

Though, the confusion is not unwarranted. The reason why search engine optimization is so tricky is that nobody actually knows the rules of the game. If you are unfamiliar with search engine optimization, basically it's attempting to up your "page rank" as compared to other websites in your same vertical.

Essentially, everybody wants to be on the first page of Google, right? If you are on the first page of Google, your visibility will go up, and more people will engage with and interact with your content.

Attempting to figure out how to optimize your website for maximum search engine ranking is exactly what search engine optimization is. It is a constant balancing act between the proprietors of websites and the search engines. As you might very well be aware, there is a lot of dross on the Internet. People use Google and other search engines to help them filter through all of the bad content to find good content. The reason why Google is such a popular resource is that it is exceptionally good at delivering high-quality content to its users.

Website owners want their websites to be seen as high quality and have search engines like Google display them to searchers who are using particular keywords. So, the idea behind effective search engine optimization is to gain a high "page rank" for specific keywords. So, for example, if your blog is about budget travel, you would be keenly interested in appearing on Google's first-page search results for the keyword "budget travel."

However, this is much easier said than done. Google keeps on purposely changing the rules of its algorithm and website owners are constantly trying to figure out these rules. For example, a few years ago website owners discovered that if they simply repeated specific keywords, these would get picked up by the Google algorithm and send their pages to the top of the list.

However, just because content constantly repeats a certain keyword does not necessarily make that content high quality. This led to a practice known as "keyword stuffing" where writers would simply try and jam in desired keywords as many times as possible. Of course, this content was very poor quality and difficult to read. After a while, Google figured this out and it changed its algorithm to punish those who produced keyword-stuffed content.

So, what does this mean for you and your blog? Basically, it's very important to stay on top of current search engine optimization trends and try to apply them to your blog. However, using search engine optimization techniques is akin to using salt in your food. You want to use enough to enhance the flavor of your food, but too much salt will make your food inedible.

Search engine optimization is much like this. You want to use some tactics to try and gain the Google algorithm to your advantage, but you do not want to use too many. Google will actually punish websites that it deems are using search engine optimization to the detriment of content (a concept known as "black hat SEO"). To keep your blog on the good side of Google, you want to use what is known as "white hat SEO" techniques.

If you are looking to get into the world of search engine optimization, we recommend that you start off with these basic tips.

Be specific about the niche of your blog

If you want your blog to naturally benefit from search engine optimization, you need to be specific about what you are actually using that blog to discuss. For example, "travel" is a huge keyword that encompasses many different topics. You will want to focus your search engine optimization attempts on things that are a bit more targeted. For another example, "budget travel" is better and more targeted, but "budget travel in Europe," or "budget travel in Croatia," are much more targeted.

Do not try and spread the focus of your blog too thinly. For example, some people may try and combine "budget travel" with "interior design." This is not a good SEO approach because those two topics have nothing at all to do with each other. It is a better practice to run multiple blogs that focus on different subjects than one blog that tries to focus on many different things.

Understand the power of linking

There are many ways that you can use links to your advantage in the search engine optimization game. Using links correctly will help your standing as an authority source within the Google framework. There are typically two different kinds of links when it comes to external websites. These links are known as "outbound links" and "inbound links."

Outbound links are where you are linking to outside sources of information. If you want to use outbound links to your best benefit, it is best practice linking to other high-ranking websites in your vertical. So, for example, if you are writing in the budget travel niche, it may be worthwhile for you to link to websites like Rick Steves or Lonely Planet.

Linking to sources that are seen by Google to be authorities in your vertical will help you seem more legitimate to Google as they prove that you have done your research and you *know* who the powerhouses are in your vertical.

Inbound links. These are when other people link to *your* site. Traditionally these are valued very highly in SEO - if people are linking to your site, it *typically* means that they are considering you an authority source. However, this is complicated; once the black hat SEOs figured out the importance of inbound links, they started out schemes where you could pay to have people link your website on absolutely random other sites. Google discovered this and promptly made the value of inbound links more convoluted.

This is an area that you typically have little control over; unless you are going black hat and paying people to link your site (not recommended), you do not have control over who is linking to your site and when most of the time. *However,* in some instances, you do have control over this, and you should take advantage of it when you do. A good example of this would be putting a guest post on somebody else's blog - if you do this, you should definitely link back to your own site. You can also link to your site by putting it in the signature of your forum or social media presences (if allowed).

The other way that you can play with links is with internal linking. That is, if you write a blog post on your blog, link to other blogs you have written or other relevant pages on your site. It's also helpful if you have pertinent lists of links on your main blog page, like your 10 most popular posts.

Your setup does matter slightly with timing and HTML

Some basic HTML tips aren't worth as much as they *used* to be in the SEO game, but they are still worth mentioning.

Use keywords. Picking the right keywords for your website is a challenging game - so much so that some web owners are known to pay thousands of dollars to have somebody pick out great keywords to optimize his or her websites. If you want to get that targeted traffic that is specifically looking for what *you* offer, you need to dig down deep and optimize for specific keywords.

There is also an art to the correct way of using keywords. Unlike what many SEO "gurus" will tell you, there actually is no "magic formula" for maximum SEO impact. If your keyword is "budget travel in Croatia," using it two or three times in a 1000-word article will probably be more than enough. You want it to sound natural. A good way to test this is to write your blog post with your keywords and give it to a friend (who isn't familiar with SEO) and ask how it sounds. Ask if they can pick out the keywords. If your friend cannot, then you have done a great job. If the keywords are painfully obvious, they will be to the reader and ultimately to Google.

Use meta tags. Meta tags are a way of embedding keywords into your actual HTML code. If you are using a platform like WordPress or Joomla, there should be a box prompting you for meta tags that does not require you using actual HTML to get them into the script. You do not want to overdo it on the meta tags, but making use of them does provide a small benefit.

Simply add your targeted keywords here, and the program will do the rest.

Make use of heading tags. Again, if you are using a blog platform like WordPress, you should see that you get options to use "headers." You should absolutely use these and put your keywords into your headers and sub-headers of your text. Not only does using headers and subheaders help break up your blog post into more consumable chunks, but it *also* gives you a boost where Google is concerned. Placing keywords inside your headers and then having them marked by header tags will flag these words as "more important" to Google and give you a bit of an edge.

Be patient

The number one takeaway about search engine optimization is that *it is going to take time*. There is absolutely no way around this fact. If you are doing the "white hat" version of SEO (meaning that you are playing by all the rules and not trying to push funny business past Google), you are going to have to wait a while to see results.

If you are reading between the lines here, you are probably thinking, "all that this chapter said was to write good content and network with others." Those are indeed the key components of SEO. If you want Google to recognize you as somebody that should be highly ranked in your niche, you actually need to *be* highly ranked in your niche by producing high-quality content and also hobnobbing with the important names in your industry.

Again, what many search engine optimization "gurus" seem to miss is that search engine optimization is actually not about trying to cheat the system. The reason why Google re-calibrates its algorithms constantly is to ensure that top quality content gets put front and center. Most "black hat" search engine optimization techniques rarely work for an extended period of time. It's not good enough to merely be on the top of the Google results for two weeks before Google figures out your game and penalizes your site. This is counterproductive.

This is just going to take time. You cannot expect SEO magic to happen overnight. But if you put the necessary amount of time into it and keep on producing great content, your traffic will increase at a slow but steady rate.

Chapter 7: Break Down of a Blogger's Income

Bloggers have several ways that they create an income through their blogs. Affiliate programs, guest posting, and display ads are some of the most commonly known ways. However, they are not often talked about in a way that truly supports beginners in understanding how to take full advantage of these advertisement opportunities.

If you truly want to generate a great income through your blog, you need to know the "behind the scenes" stuff that most bloggers do not want to openly share about on their pages because this would debunk the mystique that they keep up. It might also have a negative impact on how their current financial deals are going. So, consider this your official induction into the blogger locker room where you will learn about how these things really earn you money.

There are three ways that bloggers talk about most when it comes to making money: affiliate programs, guest posting, and advertisements. These three methods provide a great opportunity for bloggers to collaborate with other companies to create an income for themselves. Let's take a moment to explore each of these in-depth so that you can have a greater understanding of how these three methods work.

Affiliate Marketing

Affiliate marketing is a great marketing strategy that allows you to collaborate with companies who want exposure for their brands. Essentially, you blog about them and let your audience know about their products or services, and they pay you to do it. This is why you see many blogs with a disclaimer like: **"Products and services in this post may be sponsored through an affiliate program so that I can better serve you.**" This disclaimer is not only a polite way to let their readers know that they may be profiting off of the post, but also it is a legal requirement. If you will be ranking on Google searches, you must have disclaimers on all of your affiliated or sponsored posts.

There are many ways that bloggers get started with affiliate marketing. Many programs like Amazon Affiliate and ClickBank exist to support bloggers in finding these programs to join so that they can begin making an income from their blog. The nice thing about having a sponsorship program such as this is that it means you do not have to wait for companies to reach out to you to market for them. However, you need to be aware of how much you actually stand to make from these programs. For example, while Amazon Affiliate is a great starter program, you do not actually make a lot of money from them. So, while you can make **some**, if you are looking to hit $100+ days early on, this would not be a good starting point for you. Instead, consider a program that will offer you greater payouts for each referral you make.

Once you grow your audience a bit more, you can begin reaching out to companies and asking them if they would like to use you as an affiliate marketer. Alternatively, if you know of any companies that fit your niche that have built-in affiliate programs, you can apply for those as well. The more affiliate deals you are a part of, the more you stand to make, but it is important to make sure that you are nurturing each deal accordingly so that you can make funds from these deals!

Guest Posting

In the blogging world, guest posting means that you create a post for someone else's blog and they will host it for you. You can then create a post on your own blog that markets this post on their blog. Many bloggers who already have a thousand or more followers will begin offering these services, paid. Offering to guest post on someone else's blog is a great way to share your audience, as well as share your expertise with their readers. The idea here is that someone will pay you and you will write for them and then promote your writing on their blog to your own audience. This offers them the opportunity to market a unique piece of information to their audience, as well as access to your audience when you send your readers over.

While this will not necessarily be something you can do as a paid service with less than a thousand readers per month, or at least some form of established audience, it is still a great way to begin getting your audience larger. You can practice guest blogging early on as a way to expand your audience faster and then, once you have a more established audience, you can begin offering this as a service.

Advertisements

Paid advertisements are a great way to begin creating an income from your blog. On WordPress, there is a plugin you can use that will allow you to begin monetizing your blog through various paid advertisements. The most common way to do paid advertisements on a blog is through Google Ads. This plugin can easily be installed, and then you simply create an account with Google Ads and give them permission to advertise on your blog. You place specific areas on your blog where their advertisements will be shown and then every time someone clicks the ad, you are paid. This is called "pay per click."

Another way that bloggers will advertise on their page is by offering privately paid advertising packages. This allows companies with the same audience as you to pay you a fee per month and you display their ad (and their ad only) in certain places on your blogging website. These packages require more hands-on attention than Google Ads, but they do have the capacity to earn you more money per month, depending on the deal you create with the advertiser. However, these have become increasingly less common since the introduction of Affiliate Marketing, which tends to be more cost-effective for marketers.

These three primary ways ultimately make up the most common ways that virtually all bloggers create an income from their website. However, they are not the only ways available. This is just to give you a clear breakdown of where the bulk of most bloggers are earning from.

Chapter 8: Offer Additional High-Quality Content Outside Your Blog

This may seem counterintuitive; after all, if you want to drive traffic to your blog, shouldn't you be focusing mostly on your blog? The answer to this is both "yes" and "no."

However, sometimes you need to think outside the box to get the traffic you crave... or, more precisely, "think outside the blog."

A great way to make your content go further is to repurpose it. We will focus more on reproducing your content to make it either evergreen or to extend the power of a viral post in a later part of this book, but here we would like to discuss the power of eBooks and white papers with you.

While Google is extremely powerful when it comes to traffic generation and should not be ignored, another wonderful way to drive traffic to your blog is by harnessing the power of Amazon. Amazon is a powerful self-publishing platform that has tons of people who are looking for content in your niche. These people are sitting around with credit cards in their hands looking for the exact kind of content that you can offer them.

First of all, exploring what Amazon has to offer will give you an entirely new group of people to work with. Some people do not trust blogs right away and would prefer to purchase a book that is published in their area of interest. Secondly, producing a high-quality book will go very far toward making you seem like an authority in your field, and having the credentials to prove it.

While "publishing" a book may seem like a very daunting and expensive task, thanks to Amazon this could not be further from the truth. It is actually very easy and free to set up an account on Amazon and start publishing books right away. Of course, you will need to ensure that the eBooks you publish are high quality and of use to your readers. You will likely need to do more background research for a quality white paper or eBook as compared to a blog post.

However, if you put the time and effort in, you may be surprised at how far your eBook will reach. Plus, if you have a top-ranking eBook on Amazon, this will also affect your Google search results positively. People may search for your topic, and the Amazon result will come up first, with your personal blog beneath it.

To get the most out of an Amazon eBook, there are several tips and tricks that you should take into consideration.

Put an incentive in the eBook itself

Probably the most popular avenue here is to offer consumers a "free report," but this is by far not the only option. You could offer readers of your eBook access to a free course, special interviews, or any other number of additional free goodies to encourage them to visit your blog.

Make sure to link strategically within the eBook

If you are clever enough, you may be able to link to your blog within the part of your eBook that potential buyers can "preview." This means that even if the person does not purchase your eBook, they may click through to your blog anyway.

If you already have a following on your blog, use your eBook as a launch party

If you are lucky enough to already have people interacting with your content on your blog, make sure to harness this if you are publishing an eBook. A great way to get more traffic to your blog is to invite your readers to review your book. Send it to them for review, and if they have a blog, they may post a review there, and link back to *your* blog. This will give you quality inbound links. If they are excited about it, your followers may also advertise your eBook for you through social media.

Take advantage of any traffic that is gained through your eBook

The best way to do this is to create a personalized landing page so that anybody who clicks through to your blog from your eBook gets a personalized greeting. This will also help you judge how much traffic that your eBook is producing for you.

Depending on what your blog is centered around, eBooks and white papers are not the only options for this. For example, if you are a software developer, offering freeware of various sorts is also a very good way to get traffic to your blog, particularly if your freeware is considered high quality.

Chapter 9: How to Package Your Blog Ideas?

Blogging is like creating a present and giving it to someone, whether you know them or not. Of course, you want to make it as presentable as it can be in order to make them happy. One problem in creating a blog from scratch is how you will step by step organize all your ideas into one. This means that your main goal is to generate money and before you can do that, you must first do the basics. Making money as your goal would help you package your blog successfully.

What do you want to write about?

The first step is knowing what you want to write about. The best topics to blog about are topics that interest you; topics that you have sufficient knowledge in. Writing on issues that you are knowledgeable on will make your content more authentic, and it also makes planning your content a lot easier. It's also important that you actually understand the topic. If you create your blog posts based on copy-paste information you found on the internet, the audience will lose their interest in reading. Viewers always know when someone doesn't truly understand the blog topics they're discussing – and you do not want that.

So, think about the topics that come best to mind and note them all down.

Knowing the topics, you are good at will help you have ideas on what you want to write about. Finding the right content to write about will become a lot easier when you have specific details to work with. The niches are the most lucrative for those looking to monetize their blogs. You do need to keep in mind, though, that most profitable niches are very competitive. So, you need to pay extra attention to developing a strategy that works.

Find Your Niche

One term you're going to hear of often is the word "niche". "Niche" is a common buzzword in the online industry; the sooner you understand what it's about, the better. The word refers to a particular area or space you want to focus your blog on. Within that particular space, you will find an audience that is interested in the same things you'd like to blog about. In this current Digital Age, it is important that you find a niche of your own. With millions of bloggers trying to carve out the same kinds of space that you are trying to form for yourself, it's important that you stay away from trying to be generic. This will help you develop content that viewers will find useful, valuable, and/or relatable.

Finding a niche isn't an easy task, though — especially if you are a first-time blogger. You most probably have a series of ideas that you would like to share, and you aren't sure where or how to start. This is what leads most aspiring bloggers to ask, "What kind of blog should I start?"

To help you with your dilemma in finding your niche, here's a list of the 5 most profitable niches that can help you in thinking about your blog topic.

Lifestyle

A lifestyle blog is a visual representation of the author's everyday life, interests and activities. The blog will be very personalized — since the content comes from your thoughts and your actions. You will typically find quotes the author will relate to or find inspiring; pictures of areas they visited; pictures of their homes and workplaces; and reflections on the activities that went through their day. Lifestyle blogs are often created to inspire people on ways of living.

The lifestyle blogger's goal is to be seen as a go-to person when a user is trying to make decisions regarding their daily lives.

Travel

A travel blog online is often dedicated to showcasing the different destinations, across the globe which the author of the blog visits.

A travel blog is more effective when pictures are used. This is why most travel blogs found online consists of various pictures of the author's adventures. A travel blog can also be used to inform the audience on efficient ways to travel to certain destinations.

The blog doesn't have to be based on international destinations. One could start a travel blog that depicts their locality. The blog could be dedicated to giving viewers from different parts of the world an inside look into what the author's town, city, or country looks like. It will inspire the audience to consider visiting that place – which should be the goal of the blog in the first place.

The blog could be dedicated to showcasing the sights and scenery of one location in particular. For example, one could set up a blog dedicated to showcasing the sights in Switzerland, in which the blogger would upload high quality images of the scenes they came across as they traveled across Switzerland.

The purpose of the travel niche is to encourage the audience to travel to the destinations the blog covers. It can also be used to help the audience in their travels. Some blogs cover topics about trip expenses, how to travel on a budget, and other tips in traveling.

Fashion

According to a study in 2010, 50.9% of blog readers online are women. Thus, blogs about fashion have boomed as time goes by. Fashion is a major niche with diverse expressions. It is a type of blog that can showcase clothing and accessories from different type of brands. A fashion blog could be dedicated to displaying the latest fashion trends.

A fashion blog could take a personal approach as well. There's a significant number of online users who utilize their blogs for exhibiting their fashion choices. With every photo they upload, this includes the details of the clothing and accessories they are wearing – promoting the brands that they are wearing. Fashion bloggers with large followers often end up becoming ambassadors for popular clothing labels, which is also a good way to generate money.

Some fashion blogs are dedicated to showcasing clothing, accessories and trends from one particular brand. Designer labels like *Christian Louboutin, Chanel,* and *Louis Vuitton* have blogs where they promote their latest releases and their most popular products.

For someone who is thinking of using this niche as their foundation in blogging, it would be advisable to start as a fashion blogger or as someone who is promoting clothing that they have been designing and selling before they started blogging.

Health & Beauty

Topics about health and beauty became one of the most major niches in the online community. In fact, 53.3% of blog readers are 21-35 years old. People in this age group are more health conscious than other age groups. Thus, creating blogs about this niche has a large chance to create a larger audience. There are different spaces to explore in this field, especially because the health & beauty niche has a wide range of topics to talk about.

There are commercial beauty blogs that are dedicated to advertising beauty products from one particular brand or from several brands. This type of blog includes the experiences of bloggers in using the product itself.

Blogs about make-up are also a good topic to talk about, especially because a lot of brands are in the market today. Make-up artists use their blogs to showcase their skills by posting the work they have done on clients. Some make-up artists use themselves as models, applying their skills on their own faces. Others use this as a way to promote cosmetic products as ambassadors for a particular brand.

Skincare practitioners also make use of the platform to promote their products and offer advice on skincare. There are also blogs that contain tips on how to use organic products for their skin.

Blogs about health are really relevant nowadays. Especially if you are a medical practitioner who wants to start your blog, you might want to share your knowledge about health by giving tips to readers on living a healthy lifestyle. Health topics are wide too. Using this as one of your niches may allow you to create various content for your blog since it has a wide range of topics. Just make sure that you are knowledgeable in this niche in order not to mislead the readers.

Food

Food blogs are popular with Web users – since everybody loves a picture of good food. You must remember that pictures play an important role in this niche. In order to attract readers, you must first catch their eye by convincing them about the taste of the food, whether it is good or bad.

On the other hand, restaurants have resorted to use blogs as a platform to exhibit their best creations. This is with the hope that it will attract more customers. Some individuals use food blogs to exhibit their culinary skills. Such blogs are usually created with the intent to find clients, employment or to build their brand as a personal chef. Some just want to share their experiences and give tips to readers about what to eat at a certain restaurant, or where is the best place to eat on this particular place.

These are only few of the many niches you can find online. There are other niches like Sports, News, Entertainment, Business & Economics, etc. which you can also consider when thinking about the topic for your blog. It is also necessary to focus on one niche in order to make your viewers know what you really want to talk about on your blog.

Find an Inspiration

Finding an inspiration is also helpful when you don't know what to consider in creating a blog. You may find successful bloggers online and try to study how they package their blogs. Finding an inspiration doesn't mean that you will copy these famous bloggers, but you must remember to still create your own style in order to attract an audience. If readers notice that you are just copying someone's style, you may get into trouble in the future. Find a blogger that is successful in the niche that you have chosen and use this as an opportunity to develop your own style of blogging.

It is also important to remember that finding an inspiration doesn't necessarily focus on looking at other bloggers, but also looking at the niche as a whole. To elaborate this, you may read the latest updates about the niche you want to work with. Thus, this will give you an idea on what is the trending topic that people are interested in right now.

Choose the Blog Name

The blog name plays an important role in your success. Choosing the wrong blog name, in fact, can create a tremendous effect later on. Bloggers sometimes think of random names without further considering the topics that they will publish under it. This is why choosing the right blog name is important. You may use these several tips when creating a blog name.

It Should Not Be Long

Long blog names are hard to remember. Blog names should have a recall to the audience in order for them to remember you for a long time. Keep in mind that your main goal is to generate an income, and you can get this when you have a large audience for your blog. When viewers don't remember your name, they might have difficulty finding you in the internet.

Don't Be Too Specific

Being too specific in your blog name might also affect the stories you want to publish. For example, if you named your blog "Travel in America", and decided to move to France after two years, your blog won't publish the right posts for your blog name, which can confuse the readers.

Make it Catchy

Catchy doesn't mean that you are going to use numbers or special characters just to get attention. Being catchy means being cool and creating unique name that will make a recall for your audience.

Ask Your Friends or Family

Sometimes, the best ideas are from the closest people in your life. They might give you an idea of a blog name that you are not aware of. You may also share your ideas to them and take note of their opinions about it. It might be useful in the future. Remember, more brains are better than one.

Use an Online Name Generator

If you think that the first four tips are not working, you may consider using a name generator or the dictionary itself. A name generator can help you to come up with the right name for your blog.

Create Your Own Blog Calendar

One basic step in creating a blog is knowing how to organize it at first. You cannot just create a blog randomly for an unknown reason, but you have to think ahead of it. Remember that you are creating your blog package and we want you to make money from it. The benefit of creating your blog calendar is to make you consistent in blog posting. This will help you to organize your thoughts and schedule when creating an entry for your blog. You may input how many blog posts you want to create in a month and how many days you are planning to write them. You may also include the topic you want to write about for that certain month.

Creating a blog calendar is a very useful for a blog beginner. You may create simple calendar depending on how you would want it to look like. Here is an example of a blog calendar.

Now that you have packaged your blog ideas, you may proceed in creating your blog.

Chapter 10: Writing for an Online Audience

Writing for an online audience is very different from writing for an offline audience. There are a number of reasons for this, ranging from how people expect to see content presented online versus in print, and how multimedia plays into the mix. There are also factors of timing to consider.

This chapter will focus on three main areas of writing for an online audience: how to write, what to write, and when to write.

How to Write for An Online Audience

Break up the Text – One of the key differences between writing for online and writing for print is making the paragraphs shorter online. When we read a book, we have no problem with a single paragraph taking up an entire page. However, when we read online, our eyes expect a bit of a break. As such, when writing for online, try to break up the text into shorter paragraphs of no longer than three to four lines. It may seem difficult or unnatural at first if you are an experienced writer, but it will pay off in the end when you keep your readers' attention for longer.

Use Keywords – Another big difference between writing for online and writing for print is that when you write for online, you have to include keywords in your content. This is because search engines don't have brains, and unlike humans, they can only tell what you are writing about based on the words you use. As such, if you're writing about travel, you will want to use the word "travel" throughout the text of your blog posts. If you're writing a blog post with a recipe for chocolate cake, make sure to use the phrase "recipe for chocolate cake" in the text. This tells search engines what your blog posts are about so that when people type those words and phrases into, say, Google, your blog is more likely to come up in the results.

The rule of thumb is to repeat your keywords at the beginning, middle, and end of your blog post, depending on how long it is. You don't want to overdo it, as this is called "keyword stuffing" and is seen as a hallmark of spam by search engines. When in doubt, use common sense to judge whether you've included enough keywords and phrases in a blog post for a search engine to determine what you are writing about, but not so many that your blog reads like a spam website.

Search engines' algorithms have become more sophisticated in recent years, which means they are better at determining what your blog posts are about without you having to be as explicit as in the past. But it's still good to use targeted keywords throughout your posts and throughout your blog itself to ensure you have the best chance of ranking well.

Semantic search is also becoming more important, which means that search engines like Google prioritize content that answers a specific question over content that doesn't. As such, when thinking about topics and keywords for your blog posts, consider ones that provide answers.

Spell and Grammar Check – One thing that is the same for writing for online as it is for writing for print is that it is important to spell and grammar check your posts before you publish them. This is important for two reasons. First, it looks more professional if you have proper spelling and grammar on your blog, and advertisers, sponsors, and partners will be more likely to work with you if they can tell you put the time in to ensure that your content is high quality. The same goes for your readers, who will be more likely to stick around if they can actually read your content.

The second reason is that search engines have started to penalize websites with poor spelling and grammar. Those with lots of errors fall down the rankings in search results, so it's important to ensure that your content is spelled correctly and grammar checked in order to maintain and grow your search traffic.

Less is More – While there is no rule on how long or short your blog posts should be, shorter posts usually get more attention. This is partly because your readers don't have all the time in the world to read all of the blogs they follow. That's not to say that there isn't a place for long-form writing, though. Just keep in mind your readers' scarcity of time and make sure your posts are as concise as they can be for the length that you need to say what you want to say.

It's also worth bearing in mind that you should vary the length of your posts so that they don't all have the same word count. Having lots of similar content with the same word count is another indicator of spam for search engines, so make sure you don't fall into that trap. The good news is that if you're writing a high-quality blog with original, creative content, you won't need to worry too much about this.

Don't Duplicate Content – Speaking of content, one of the biggest mistakes I see new bloggers make is duplicating content without realizing that they shouldn't. What I mean by duplicating content is publishing the same content on your site more than once, or publishing the same content on your blog and another site. Many new bloggers get excited about a great post they've written and try to shop it around to other sites to get it syndicated or republished. The problem with this strategy is that search engines see duplicate content as spam, and end up leaving the content on both sites out of the search results.

To avoid this problem, just change 20% or more of the text before republishing your content on a different page of your blog or asking another site to republish it. Move paragraphs around, use different adjectives, and add or remove sentences here and there, and you'll be fine.

Add Visual Elements – In addition to breaking up the text into shorter paragraphs, you will also want to break it up with visuals. When we read in print, we don't necessarily expect to see photos, videos, graphics, or other multimedia elements. But when we read online, we expect the text to be broken up with visuals. As such, try to include images, videos, or graphics of some kind between each paragraph, or at least after every few paragraphs.

Some industries lend themselves better to visuals than others, so if you blog about things like food, travel, fashion, or beauty, you will be at an advantage here. But even if you don't cover topics that lend themselves to visuals, try to get creative about integrating visual content. For example, if you're a finance blogger you can add graphs or charts, or if you're a tech blogger you can add graphics or infographics.

If you can do this successfully, your blog might even become as well known for its non-written content as it is for its written content. My blog started out as all text, and over time I started adding images. Now my blog is better known for photography than writing, and my readers regularly email me to tell me that they keep coming back to my blog because of the pictures.

You can also get creative with your images, stitching several together to form a collage or putting text over them to encourage people to pin them on Pinterest (Pinterest pins with text on the images tend to perform well and drive lots of traffic to blogs, so many bloggers include an image with text over it in each blog post). You can do this with software like Photoshop or online with tools like PicMonkey or Canva.

If you're blogging about something that lends itself to visuals, your readers will expect to see your own photos (or photos of you) on your blog and social media channels. As such, it is important to invest in your photography skills when you start out. You don't necessarily need to spend a lot of money on an expensive camera, but you should learn how to use the one you have (even if it is your phone) and get some editing software to touch up your photos before you publish them.

When adding visuals, keep in mind that size matters. Use the largest possible size you can (without compromising the quality, of course) so that your images, videos, and other media fill up the whole width of the body area of your blog. People like to see large images, and leaving dead white space on either side of an image is wasting an opportunity to fill the frame with the whole image.

That said, large images often come with equally immense file sizes. This can slow down the speed at which your blog loads, which search engines don't like. If you find that your file sizes are getting too big, you can install a plugin (depending on which blogging platform you use) or use software on your computer to reduce the file sizes before uploading your images.

It's also worth mentioning that it is important make sure that you have permission if you use any images, graphics, videos, or other visual content that you didn't create yourself. All too often, new bloggers use photos or images from other blogs or websites without asking permission first, and that's a big mistake. Many images and other visual content online are copyrighted, and you can make enemies (or even find yourself in legal trouble) quickly if you use content without the owner's permission.

If you don't have images or visuals of your own, there are ways to source them cheaply and easily. The most basic way is to ask the owner of an image or website if they will grant you permission to use their content. When you contact them, make sure to ask how they would like to be credited.

You can also buy stock photography and other images from websites like Picfair, or find images on sites like Flickr that are licensed under the Creative Commons. This type of license allows you to use images (and other content) for free as long as you credit the owner in the way they specify on the photo's page.

Give Them Somewhere to Go – Another thing that is important in writing for an online audience is making sure to give your audience somewhere to go at the end of each of your blog posts. What I mean by this is that when a reader comes to the end of your post, they should be presented with a number of options for other things to read and/or ways to engage with what they've just read.

The reason for this is that it benefits you to keep your readers on your blog for as much time as possible. Search engines look at how long your readers stay on your blog every time they visit in order to determine how high (or low) quality your blog is. The longer your readers stay, the higher quality your blog looks. The shorter, the lower. This makes sense, as people tend to spend more time on sites that offer relevant, high-quality information and less time on sites that offer irrelevant, poor-quality information.

In order to keep your readers on your site for as long as you can, there are a few things you can do. One is having a "You may also like" section at the end of each post (you can do this with a plugin if you're on a platform like WordPress.org). This automatically shows thumbnail images and titles of related posts on your blog that the reader may want to look at given their similarity to the one they just read.

Another is by having social sharing buttons at the end of your posts. This not only allows readers to engage with your content, but also spreads the word about your blog posts to their social media followers.

A third is to have a comments section at the end of each post. This gives your readers a chance to share their thoughts and feedback with you, and encourages them to return to see what you and others have said in response to their comment.

There are all kinds of other things you can add to your blog to keep people on your site, so be creative about using plugins or other tools to give your readers a reason to stay.

Allow Comments –We no longer live in an era where we push information out to our audience and give them no way to respond to or interact with what they read. In an increasingly digital world, people are used to being able to share their thoughts and opinions immediately after reading something, whether in a comment on a blog post or on social media. As such, allowing comments gives your readers a way to engage with your content and create a connection with you as a blogger that will keep them coming back for more.

There are a few things to remember when allowing comments on your blog. The first is to make sure to moderate them (you can set this up in the settings section of your blogging platform). Don't publish a comment on your blog until you have screened it and approved it. This is partly because of spam (unfortunately spammers love to leave nonsensical comments on blog posts with lots of spammy links in them). If your readers start to see lots of spam comments on your blog, it will turn them off to reading it and they won't want to leave comments themselves. Moderating your comments shows that you care about your readers having a good user experience, and that you are willing to put the time in to ensure quality comments.

The other reason to moderate your comments is that you will occasionally get people leaving rude or offensive comments on your blog. While some bloggers choose to publish these comments in the name of free speech, most realize that people that leave comments like this are not interested in having a debate or dialogue with you; they are only out to disparage you. Trying to respond to their comments usually just encourages them to continue leaving ever more vicious comments. As such, most bloggers choose not to publish them in the first place.

The next thing to remember when allowing comments is to make it easy for your readers to leave a comment. This is an area where I see a lot of bloggers—even professional ones—make mistakes. If you are going to moderate your comments (which you should), there's no reason to make your readers check a box or enter a captcha to ensure they're not a spammer, or do a math problem before they can hit the "send comment" button. At best, it's irritating, and at worst, it's a deterrent from leaving a comment at all.

The third thing to remember about comments is to allow your readers to comment from as broad a range of logins as possible. This is another place where many bloggers fail. Again, if you're going to moderate your comments, why force people to log in with Facebook, Twitter, Disqus, WordPress, or something similar? Many people don't have the required login or don't want to leave a comment via a profile, and these requirements turn them off from commenting. As such, make sure to always give the option of just a name and email address (the latter not published publically) so that anyone can leave a comment. You will get far more comments this way.

What to Write Online

Once you know how to write for an online audience, you have to decide what to write for your readers. This can be easier for some people than others, as it depends on how many ideas you have and what topic(s) you want to write about. There are a few best practices when you sit down to think about what you will blog on, so make sure to consider the following before you start.

Find a Niche – When I started blogging back in 2002, there were very few blogs out there and most people had never heard of blogging. Even when I started A Lady in London in 2007 there weren't a lot of blogs around. As such, I had the benefit of being able to be a generalist. I write about London, travel, and lifestyle, and I don't always specialize in any particular area.

Fast-forward to today, and new bloggers have a lot more competition. With millions of blogs out there, it's much harder to make a name for yourself as a blogger than it was five or ten years ago.

As such, many people choose to focus on a niche area in order to get known faster. While you don't have to do this, it will definitely help you become an authority in your space more quickly than if you choose to be a generalist.

For example, I have a friend that started a travel blog a number of years ago. Instead of focusing on general travel, he decided to blog only about travel in the mountains. From skiing to mountain biking, he covered anything related to mountain travel, but nothing else. As a result of specializing in one area of travel, he became known in the industry very quickly and was able to start building partnerships almost from the beginning.

That said, I never want to make people feel like they have to find a niche. If you want to be a generalist, you should. But if you do, make sure you know exactly what sets your blog apart from all the other generalist blogs out there. The more specific and clear you can be, the better your audience and partners will understand why they should come to your blog instead of someone else's.

List Ideas – Another thing to do when you start out is to list your ideas for blog posts. If you can get to 10 or 20 without too much trouble, you probably have enough content for a blog. If you can only get to five, you probably need to widen your focus to include some other areas or topics.

Steadily Source Ideas – Along those lines, it is important to steadily source ideas for new blog posts as you check your original ideas off your list. There's nothing worse than realizing that you need to publish a blog post the next day and you don't have any idea what to write about. This is particularly true if, like me, you only write about things or places you have experienced firsthand. In order to prevent this from happening, it's a good idea to keep a running list of blog post ideas that you can draw from if you're ever stuck.

Editorial Calendar – Furthermore, having an editorial calendar can be an even bigger help. If you know you're going to blog twice a week on Monday and Thursday, keep a calendar (I use my Gmail calendar) and make sure that you have blog post topics lined up several weeks into the future at all times. This will allow you to anticipate what you are going to write about, how much time it will take, and what you might need to do in order to write about it (for example, cook a meal if you're going to write a recipe post, or take pictures of a museum if you're going to write a review of it).

That said, don't be so rigid with your editorial calendar that you miss out on covering events or topics that are trending on a given day. One of the most powerful things about blogging is its immediacy, so if something comes up that is relevant to write about, feel free to push less time-sensitive posts to future dates (or feel free to even publish out of cycle).

When to Write Online

Once you've decided what you're going to write about, you need to decide when to write about it. I recommend writing no less than once a week, although I know some people that work full-time struggle to meet this kind of quota. The more you post, the more traffic you will get, both from loyal readers and from search engines.

If you can post more frequently, you will see your traffic grow faster and you will have more content to point people to when they visit your blog. I know one professional blogger that tells new bloggers to post every single day even if it's just a quick update.

How often you post is ultimately up to you. But regardless of the frequency, you'll need to consider a few things about the timing. The first is what day(s) of the week to post. In many industries, there are days of the week when people are more likely to be online reading blogs. Whatever your subject, a quick Google search should bring up a wealth of content about what day is the best one for you to publish your posts. Doing so on that day will ensure you get the maximum exposure and traffic for your content. Even if you can't write during that day, it's worth writing something beforehand and scheduling your post to go live on the day it will get the most visibility.

In addition to there being better days and worse days of the week to post content on your blog, there are also better and worse times of day. For example, in some industries (think finance), people read blogs early in the morning to get a feel for what will happen that day. In others, it's the middle of the day or the evening. If you do some research on what time of day is the best for your topic, you will have the best chance of getting the most traffic to your blog that day.

The same goes for time zones. If your entire audience is in your home country, you'll have a pretty easy time deciding when to publish your blog posts. But if your audience is global, you will have to take that into account when you choose which time zone is ideal to publish your posts for.

Chapter 11: How Often Should You Blog?

The simple answer to this question is as often as possible. It is important that you blog at regularly timed intervals.

To the minute if you can

That way, people will be waiting for your next blog to arrive. It is akin to waiting for your newspaper or magazine to be delivered. If you are going to post daily, do it at the same time every day and make sure people know this. Mention it in your blogs, mention it on your page that you will be posting at 11 AM (or whatever time you choose) every weekday. If you are posting weekly or monthly, do the same thing.

Be consistent and keep to that schedule. If you choose to go off schedule, let people know. There is nothing wrong with going off schedule for special occasions or events. For example, you might be a music blogger who attends the Burning Man festival in Nevada, which runs for seven or eight days. You may choose to blog every day from there. I guarantee you if you have an audience, they will love it. However, blogging every day is both time-consuming and, to start with, probably not necessary.

Most magazines, whether online or in print don't come out every day, but once a week or monthly. You might want to start by making a commitment to blog once a week, at the same day and time. This gives you a week to think about the material and the presentation, to write it, to edit it, and to make it the best it can be when it finally goes online. The great news is, WordPress has a facility that helps you plan the content and release dates of your articles.

I have used the once a week blog as an example, and it is a very common interval for blogging, but your blog scheduling should be dictated by the market you are in and the demand from your readers. To help decide, you might want to ask yourself some questions before you start blogging.

1. What are your goals in terms of your content?

To start with you might want to just gain a reputation.

Maybe you want to build up an email circulation list. Perhaps you want people to read your blog with a view to hiring you as a freelance writer. These goals can dictate how many times you need to blog. Blogging once or twice a week might be the way to go. Twice a week can make quite a difference, particularly if you are trying to build a positive reputation. It all comes back to how well you know your target market.

If you are writing a blog every day without knowing your target audience, in the hope that some people will see it and respond to your content, you might be peddling incredibly hard for little reward. But if you know exactly what your target is all about and your blogs reflect that, then you will have a clearer grasp on how responsive your readers will be to two blogs a week.

2. How many blogs have you already published?

Statistics show that the more blogs you have on your website, the more visitors you have. Let me put a caveat on that. The more good quality blogs you have on your website, the more visits you have. Let us think about that. More great blogs leads to more visitors. More visitors leads to better sales, or clicks, or work, take your pick from your strategy. In short, more blogs leads to more income. If you can, therefore, blog more than once a week, at least to start with, you are, in the medium to long-term, doing yourself a massive favor. But importantly, don't sacrifice the quality of your blog for quantity. You will do your reputation, and your blog traffic, a disservice.

3. Where are people reading your blogs?

I am talking about differentiating between your own website and the social networks you subscribe to. You need to work out the difference between how many people view your blog on your own website, and how many on Facebook, Twitter, etc. Some websites get most of their traffic from search engines like Google, and others get most of their traffic from social media sites. If search engines are your major source, you may not need to blog quite as much, but if it is social networks, you may want to consider blogging more often.

Ultimately, make sure you are keeping track of all this information, and WordPress helps you with that as well. It is vital to working out what you publish, when you publish it, and where you publish it. I hope you are getting a feel for the fact that you may need to experiment and solicit feedback from your readers in terms of the frequency of your blog.

Other Tips

Work out how much time you can devote to writing high-quality blogs. I repeat to the point of tedium, don't sacrifice the quality of your blogs in return for quantity. There is no more surefire way of driving away either existing readers or potential new readers than by producing crap blogs on a regular basis. It is a lethal combination. People want high-quality content, content that resonates with them and can help them with their issues. Always keep this in mind. If, due to time constraints, you are unable to produce more than one blog a week then so be it.

Make sure it is an absolute humdinger

Down the line, you may be able to free up more time to write more, or you may look at networking and introducing guest spots on your blog. As long as the quality is high. Establish reader (customer) demand. Let us say you have all the time in the world, you love writing blogs, and they are on point and high quality. They speak to your customers directly.

This does not necessarily mean you should blog every day. It is entirely possible that your customers will not want to read a daily blog. If somebody is on an email list and you send them an email every day about your blog, it could be seen as intrusive. However, you will not know until you try it. Experiment, start with one a week, then two, then three and see what happens. Also, survey your customers, ask them what they want.

Experiment with content.

Depending, obviously, on your niche, and how you generate income, you may want to try different blogs to see what impact on traffic and feedback they have. You may just try the purely informative blogs, heavy on deep quality writing. You may try blogs which heavily advertise products or services.

See what happens

You may want to do a bit of both and see what happens as you experiment again. Don't forget, you're looking at two different things. You are looking at blog traffic, and also conversion rates, i.e., how many readers buy something or click on affiliate advertisements, or whatever it is.

In conclusion, with these experiments, there are three potentially competing elements to consider. Firstly, the amount of traffic you want to generate. Secondly, the amount of income you want to generate. Blogs that are heavy on selling may have higher conversion rates to sales, but a much lower number of people reading them. You need to find a happy middle ground. Finally, it is how much time you can spare.

Don't over commit, please don't. You will burn out very quickly and become disillusioned. When you start you will be tentative and hesitant about what you are doing, this is natural. You will become more confident as you go along and quicker at what you do. Remember, don't sacrifice quality over quantity and don't over-stress yourself.

Blogging and search engine optimization

Blogging has been shown to significantly boost ranking in searches. That is, if the blog posters use good SEO tactics. It is not just the keywords that increase the power of the search results, it is also frequency. So, if your blogging high-quality SEO proficient regular blogs you will see search results improve on a progressive basis.

One Final Tip – About Archived Blogs

Don't underestimate the power of your archived blogs. Make them easily accessible. Research has shown that you can get many sales or conversions from your historical blogs, in fact, probably more if you have a bank of high-quality blogs.

Think about it.

If you have new visitors who have subscribed to your email list and read your blog on a regular basis, it shows that they like your stuff. They are highly likely to dig back into old blogs.

Therefore, don't just forget them. Review them regularly and potentially edit them to make them more powerful sales tools for you.

Chapter 12: Forming a Blog Monetization Strategy

Your blog monetization consists of the various business aspects of your blog. To create a blog monetization strategy, you need to think like a businessman. Stop looking at your blog from the perspective of a blogger.

There are various steps that you can take in coming up with the best blog monetization strategy.

Identifying What the Market Wants

Earlier in this book, we discussed the niche selection process with a focus on building a blog around your interests and passions. Considering this aspect when developing the blog is crucial. In selecting a niche, you have to go beyond identifying your passion. It is vital that you also look at the type of market you are getting into. What this entails is you looking at the various niches in an industry you have an interest in.

What is the audience in the various niches searching for? What outcomes do they desire? How large is the market? A blog that will earn a lot of money must be able to offer its readers a specific outcome. If you don't understand this vividly, then assume you have an interest in finance. In the finance industry, your blog can fall into the personal finance niche.

This is a niche that has a broad audience always in search of new information to save money, invest, and control their spending. The information they are searching for are the outcomes you can offer. In your monetization strategy, you can focus on providing tips, online courses, and a spreadsheet that assists your readers in creating and following a budget. From this point, you can go into other areas like the best investment options and how to save money the right way.

The outcome of the blog will be an improvement in the personal finance of the readers. This outcome is the product you are selling, and readers are always searching to buy this product.

Expanding Your Sources of Incoming Traffic

Monetizing your blog will only be effective if there is constant traffic to your blog. Regardless of the number of loyal audience members you currently have, there is a need to attract new audience members. You don't expect the same audience members to keep purchasing the same product over and over.

To improve the traffic to your blog, you must be willing to explore other sources. Twitter, YouTube, Instagram, LinkedIn, Facebook, Reddit, and several other social platforms are excellent sources of blog traffic. The content formats can also vary in the same manner. Posting videos, images, and podcasts; using paid advertising; and incorporating search engine optimization (SEO) all play a crucial role in generating the right amount of traffic to your blog.

Developing the Hub of the Business

In developing a monetization strategy, you have to pay close attention to your blog. You must transform it from a basic blog where you share opinions to one on which the content of each post is curated with a goal. The goal of the content is to generate conversions from your blog visitors.

This means offering the best you can to make people see the blog as one with value. The blog becomes an environment for content marketing. It is from this hub that you diversify into other forms of marketing. There are steps you must take to optimize your blog for lead generation and conversions.

The first is getting them to sign up on your email list through value, lead magnets, and an opt-in form. You will also need chatbots and autoresponders to work on generating these leads. To simplify this process, the goal of this hub (your blog) at this point is to convert that random stranger on your blog to a blog subscriber.

You must also be willing to engage in other actions like retargeting. This will enable your paid advertising strategies to pay off. If a visitor opens your page once and closes it, they will forget the name of the site in a few hours. Retargeting is a way of reminding them of the name and existence of your blog.

Now you can reach those visitors who didn't subscribe on the first visit. Imagine how many potential customers you will lose without this option. There are various options when you want to implement the retargeting strategy. These include Google and Facebook. This is how you develop your blog into a business hub. It focuses on capturing every visitor to make it easy to turn them into paying customers.

Leads Acquisition

A monetization strategy must include a way to get your visitors to show interest in what you are selling. Anyone who can indicate this interest in your product is a lead.

So how do you identify a lead? A person who shows interest in your business will perform any of the following actions:

- Place a call to your business
- Interact with your business through live chat, chatbot, and any other chat option
- Enroll for your webinar
- Become an email list subscriber
- Complete a free test or quiz

For a visitor to take any of these actions, it is an indication that they want to get to know you, and it is an opportunity for you to get to know them.

It is up to you to make the most of this opportunity. This is the build-up of gaining a potential customer, and you must build a stable relationship.

As mentioned in the chapter discussing email marketing, you need to offer a lead magnet for this purpose.

An opt-in form is also essential. Remember to place the forms at a position that it is easy to get the attention of the lead.

Sales Generation

Your strategy must include a sales generation aspect. This is how you make money from the blog. These include the product page on your blog. For most blogs (including yours), this page only becomes relevant after getting a visitor to become a lead.

If you are familiar with the term "sales funnel," that is what this aspect is all about. The design of this funnel must move your leads from top to bottom effectively. This is the point at which they become customers.

Your funnel might include multiple offers of different prices or a single offer for your readers. The cheapest offer, which you can call the front-end offer, is there to get you a customer. It comes at a price that a lead can pay without feeling it much.

The next offer, which is your core offer, can be a consultation service, training course, or membership site. The final offer is the high-end offer, which yields the most profit for you. This can be affiliate products, coaching, or follow-up sales.

To effectively move your leads down the sales funnel, you need to implement the use of an autoresponder sequence in addition to your retargeting strategies. You prepare these emails in advance and have them sent to your leads at a later date.

Growing Your Community

This is the final step in the monetization strategy, and it is an outcome of your long-term thinking. The idea here is simple. What if a lead doesn't buy from you?

There is no need to be bitter about this. The future is always full of surprises. To prepare for these surprises, you must solidify your relationship with these leads. That is why you need to have a community. It is through this community that you can continue to provide value to your leads.

There are various ways to grow your community. It can be through email newsletters, blog content, podcasts, social media updates, videos, live chat, and many more. Consistency is vital, and it will surely pay off later.

How Much Can You Make Blogging?

The amount you make blogging is dependent on your effort. Placing a figure on this amount will be impossible. Different blogs attract different individuals. Despite these facts, you can surely get a range when determining your possible income from blogging. To give you this range, there is a look at how much several popular bloggers make every month.

This gives you an insight into how much you can make from blogging. On the list (Dizon, 2019), the top-paid blogger earns as much as $125,000 per month. On the same list, the lowest-earning blogger makes at least $1,500 per month. These figures are just an estimate and should only serve as a guide.

Chapter 13: Mindset in Your Goals

You have your blog created, your website is finished, and now we are going to get to the most important information. Your mindset in the goals that you have are going to be what either makes or breaks your success. If you are approaching this like a business and you are treating it like something that you value, you are going to be successful. Being in the right frame of mind with the right mindset is going to help you in the long run.

If you are not setting goals or building a business, you are going to see failure. The most successful people in the blogging industry have goals that they set for themselves and their business.

Growth Mindset

A growth mindset is simply referring to how you view your skills and your abilities. If you feel that your skills and abilities are something that you were born with and you cannot prove, then you have a fixed mindset. On the other hand, if you believe that your skills and your abilities are something that you can learn and grow, then you have a growth mindset. In business, a growth mindset is important. In blogging, a growth mindset is vital. It's important to know that you are not required to be a complete expert in the industry that you choose, all that you need is passion. That passion is going to drive you to want to learn more about the topic that you've chosen.

Consider an example of an individual who chooses the topic of business. They find that business is too broad of a topic, so they focus on freelancers and entrepreneurs. They themselves are in an entrepreneur because they've started a blog. When they began, they made of had a good background in what they were writing on, but they were not an expert. This individual has a passion for small businesses, freelancers, and entrepreneurs, which is going to drive them to follow the latest trends that affect these areas and write about them.

Another example to consider would be a mother who has a passion for helping other young mothers through the difficult years of raising children. This mother may have never gone to college, may never have held a high-power position, and may have been a stay-at-home mother for the last decade. This mother has a passion for sharing the life hacks that she's learned over the last ten years, and as a result, she is going to be effective at blogging in the parenting niche. You are not required to take college courses to write a blog. The only requirement is that you have the desire to learn and grow as an individual.

Adopting a growth mindset is easier than you may think. It starts with the first beginning to reframe your thought processes and focusing on the positive. When you focus on the positive, you are giving yourself the chance to brush off any negativity that is going to hold you back. Each time you come face-to-face with an obstacle, rather than giving up, refocus your thoughts, and reframe how you view the obstacle. Each obstacle in your life is nothing more than an opportunity for growth and advancement. When you recognize this, you are going to understand that anything is possible.

Tips to Develop A Growth Mindset

Be Grateful

When you are acknowledging what you have, you are having a powerful influence over your outlook on life. Keep a gratitude journal and record everything that you are grateful for because when you do this, you are opening your mind up to positivity. Once you change your outlook on life, you're going to see the power of positive thinking can have.

Make Success Choice

Being successful is a choice. You need to choose success, or you will never achieve it. Look at the tendencies and ways that you are holding yourself back and develop a plan to change that. When you are aware of your self-sabotaging behaviors, you understand what you need to change.

Obstacles Are Not Problems

Viewing an obstacle is a challenge rather than a problem that is going to help your mindset. By seeing the obstacle as nothing more than a learning opportunity and a way to challenge yourself, you are going to see better results and outcomes. Obstacles often hold us back, but that does not need to be the case. When you change your mindset and how you view these obstacles, you are going to see your success skyrocket.

Enjoy the Journey

Often, we assume that the end result is the successful completion of the task. More often than not, the journey is more important than our outcome. When you learn to enjoy the journey and appreciate it if you are going to see your outcomes improve. Your goal should be to learn and not successfully complete each and every endeavor that you take on.

Make A Point to Celebrate

When you make a point to celebrate your wins, you are acknowledging the success that you have already achieved. Keep in mind that when you celebrate, it's not a time to stop what you are doing, but rather it is an opportunity to reflect and continue on.

Embrace Your Imperfections

When you acknowledge your weaknesses, you'll be a better chance of using them and developing them into strengths. If you never acknowledge your weaknesses, you will never make progress in overcoming them.

Try A Different Tactic

If something isn't working, reevaluate and try something new. It's important to reflect on your processes to determine which ones are working and which ones aren't. Abandon the ones that aren't and focus on finding tactics that do work.

Failing Needs to Become Learning

To fail is to learn. Each failure that you experience needs to become a learning opportunity. This is important if you are expanding and growing. Part of a growth mindset is learning from setbacks.

You Only Need to Your Own Approval

Make it a priority to stop seeking approval from others. By seeking approval outside of yourself, you are constantly going to feel that you are not good enough and you are going to feel like you have failed. Set your goals and compare them against what do you want to achieve.

Find Your Purpose

If you find your purpose, you are going to be happier. You are also going to find that it is easier to tackle problems and obstacles if you are working within your purpose.

Growth Is More Important Than Speed

Life is not a race, and you do not need to finish first. It is more important to grow then it is to achieve something quickly.

Improvement and Failure to Not Go Hand-In-Hand

If you hear the phrase room for improvement, do not assume that you are feeling at something. Room for improvement just means that you have another chance to grow as an individual.

Practice Mental Toughness

You need to learn to reshape criticism and your response to it.

Start Using the Word Yet

Every time you struggle with the tax, it's important that you just remember you have not mastered it yet. Yet is the keyword and leaves room to grow and improve.

Learn from The Mistakes of Others

By looking at how others have made mistakes, you are avoiding the same mistakes and giving yourself even more opportunity to grow. The key aspect of the growth mindset is that you are also using the mistakes of others, not just your own.

Create New Goals

Every time you accomplish a goal, set out to create anyone.

Take Ownership for Your Attitude

Part of developing a growth mindset means that you are owning your attitude. If you have a negative attitude, you need to become aware of it and make changes.

Blogging Is A Business

Running a blog is just like running a business because it is a business. Each aspect of the blog requires planning, execution, and follow-up. Your editorial calendar is going to be your planning as well as any research that you may do. The execution is when you write the posts, and you make them live. Follow-up comes from analyzing the statistics and making changes to your content accordingly.

Since blogging is a business, it's a good idea to consider writing a business plan before you begin. Blogging business plans are a good idea because they help you focus on what you're trying to accomplish, you become familiar with your values, and you know the direction that you would like to take. When you research business plans for blogs, you may be able to find a template or two that will assist you. If you're not, below, you will find all of the items that are needed in a blogging business plan.

Chapter 14: Common Mistakes in Blogging

New and pro bloggers alike are not immune from mistakes when blogging. So many bloggers find themselves making mistakes here and there. The key is recognizing when you've made those mistakes and correcting them. With how often the internet and people's interests change, you can find yourself slipping up at any point in your blogging career.

Here are some common mistakes bloggers make and what you can do to avoid them.

Do Not Clutter Your Site

Have you ever been to a website where there was stuff everywhere? Like a dirty kid's room, they have ads and banners and videos and pictures scattered all over the home page. Music starts playing from some ad and you can't figure out which ad it's coming from. You know there are blog posts in there somewhere, but you are afraid to click on one because it may just be another ad. Or it may lead you to another page that is just as unappealing as the home page.

This happens all the time to newer bloggers. They want to sell ad space, but also want to fill their sidebars, headers, and footers with as much information or advertisements as possible. I get it too, you want to make money right away and you have been told by other bloggers to put this here and that there. But remember, clutter is unattractive and will only drive away readers. No one wants to see a ton of ads or even too many links or side notes on your page. Keep it simple and clean. If you must have ads, only use some that are related to your blog so that they aren't so distracting.

The focus of your blog should be the blog! Ads are background noise both literally and figuratively. Too much background noise is distracting and takes away from the enjoyable content of your site. On that note, don't use ads that automatically play music or commercials when readers view your site. Have you ever visited a site that had a video automatically start playing? Not only is it annoying because you are being forced to listen and watch something instead of reading what you went to the site to read in the first place, but the entire site slows to a crawl. Those video ads that automatically play slow down websites so much. You will lose readers before they even get a chance to view any of your content. Don't use those ads.

Color Schemes and Fonts

When customizing your blog, it can be tempting to change the screen color to black with a bright yellow font. Yes, we all remember the Myspace days when that was fun to do. But society is on computers all the time now and the screens are hard enough on our eyes. Don't make it worse by using dark screens with a bright font. Darker screens cause more eye strain, and the bright fonts are awful to read. *All About Vision* recommends that you should be reading screens that are the same brightness of the room you are in, and using screens with a white background and black font. The same article also recommends looking away from your computer every twenty minutes, so make sure your pages are also to the point.

Even if you are using a white background, do not use bright lettering! Stick to darker fonts as they are easier to read. Look at amateur sites where the screen is bright white, and the font is bright green. It hurts to look at. People need darker colors to make focusing easier. If your font is too bright, no one will want to read your post.

Fonts need to be legible. I shouldn't have to explain this one, but make sure your words are easy to read. There are so many fonts out there that are fun to use and still look good.

Do Not Plagiarize

This sounds so simple until you realize how easy it is to plagiarize without even knowing you're doing it! Plagiarizing consists of writing content that is too close to some else's or is exactly what someone else wrote. It also consists of using images that are not your own. Now, here is why so many bloggers are guilty of plagiarism and don't even realize it.

Bloggers tend to plagiarize images the most. They do a search for certain images and choose one that works for their post. Then they download it and plug the image into their blog post. They credit the source and leave it at that. It sounds good, and after all, we do it on Pinterest all the time, right? Well, this is still considered plagiarism. You cannot use someone else's image without permission! Even if you cite the source within your post, you are plagiarizing as long as you do not have written consent from the original owner to use the image.

If you find images you really want to use, you are going to have to start getting permission. You can most definitely reach out to people and ask for permission, but this can be time-consuming. Many successful bloggers use stock images to remedy this problem.

Stock images are images that have been sold to companies to use without the original owner's permission. They give their rights to pictures up so that others can use the images. There are a number of sites that have stock images you can use for your site. Free sites such as *Pexels.com* offer tons of images that you can get for free. This can work well if you are on a fixed budget for now.

Bigger sites like *Shutterstock* and *Getty Images* have even more images you can use, but you will have to pay for the images. And you will still need to credit the site with your photo. The benefit of paying for images is that you can get a lot of quality images without having to worry about plagiarism. The downside is that these images are not cheap. You may wind up paying a lot of money to these sites for their images. Of course, when you are making a lot of money with your blog, you won't mind dishing out some for images.

Another way to avoid plagiarizing images it to create your own. Hire a photographer or learn how to take good photos. *Photographylife.com* has great tips on how to better your photography skills. Learning how to take great photos will save you from having to search for images on those stock images sites. Take pictures of everything. If you have a camera, bring it everywhere. If not, your phone will most likely have a camera and I am sure you rarely put your camera down. Take photos often and learn how to edit them.

There are tons of apps now that will help you to edit photos. Some are free and others you have to pay for. Remember, though, that you get what you pay for. Many bloggers love *PicMonkey*. They have a free option and a paid subscription. Naturally, you can do much more with the paid version. PicMonkey can be easier to use if you are new to editing and offers many tools in order to create your perfect images. *Photoshop* is another great photo editing service that many bloggers use. Get to know it and you will start to create great images that you don't need permission to use!

For your words, you are going to want to check to make sure they haven't already been said by someone else. There are a number of sites on the internet that will check your work for you. Sites such as *smallseotools.com* and *paperrater.com* offer free plagiarism checks for your content. All you have to do is copy and paste.

Plagiarism is never okay, even if you didn't know you were doing it. If you think that you have accidentally plagiarized someone else's images or work, please do yourself a favor and fix it. Even if you think no one will notice, just get it fixed. Somewhere down the line when you are way more popular, someone may notice that you used an image without permission, and you don't want all that legal hassle.

Don't Use Big Words

Look, we all know you're smart. You started a blog and know a lot about your niche. But you don't need to use huge words or try to make yourself smarter. Using too much technical writing will either confuse readers or bore them. We aren't in high school anymore and no one wants to read a term paper again! Write as if you are talking to a friend in a language you would use in a normal conversation. Keeping it light and easy will keep your readers engaged.

Back Up Your Information with Sources

You may have a lot to say on a subject, and that's great! But how do your readers know that you know what you are talking about? Blathering on and on about something will hold no merit if you can't back up what you are saying. So, you think calicos are the best cats and write you wrote an entire post about why they are the best. Readers may like the post, but they are going to want to know why you think calicos are the best. What are your reasons for this opinion? What evidence do you have that backs up your claim?

Readers want to know where your information comes from. Be sure to cite sources throughout your post where it needs it. Get to know hyperlinks and use them throughout the post. This gives readers a link to the information you used so they can look into it themselves.

Don't Focus on Perfecting Your Blog

So many bloggers make the mistake of aiming for perfection. They overanalyze every aspect of their blog from images to posts to editing. Your work doesn't have to be perfect! Quit spending so much time tweaking and making sure everything is just right. You are human, your readers are human, and they want to see how human you are. Let there be little mistakes, let there be little goofs. It's humorous and shows the genuine, personal side of you. Don't worry about getting every joke right, and getting the wording just right. You will drive yourself crazy perfecting your posts. At some point, you need to settle for what you have and post it.

Conclusion

Guess what? Blogging is a job! You're not just going to get there sitting on your behind waiting for something to happen, you're going to have to take massive action! The fact is, that if you're not motivated to make something happen, and if you're not blogging with the belief that whatever you're blogging about is the greatest thing to happen to the human race since the invention of fire, then you've got a sense of purpose problem.

You have basically got to believe with a sense of purpose, 100%, that what you're blogging about is absolutely critical. And you have to believe it deeply, with every single fiber of your being at the most extreme level, because if you don't buy the load of crud that you're peddling, then no one else will either. Therefore, if your blog isn't absolutely spectacular by your own standards, then you'd better either make it spectacular, or tear the whole thing down and build a better beast.

The bottom line is that you've got to believe and utterly love your blog, as if it were the most sacred thing in the universe! If you're just not seeing your blog that way, then you have to make tweaks, either to your blog, or to how you view of your blog, until you are seeing things that way.

The big money bloggers all have a sense of purpose, and completely love their blogs! Therefore, so should you! You have a mission and you need to embrace it: your mission is to help your readers with your knowledge. Embrace that and it'll help you write passionately on the subject matter that you specialize in. This sets the difference between a mediocre blogger and a successful one; the former posts just to kill time while the latter does it to connect, share, help and contribute to their audience. So, cultivate the right mindset; only then will you see positive results. Then nothing will stop you and you'll be determined not just to share but to receive what you deserve in exchange.

The monetization mindset is being aware that through blogging, you have the chance to make an exchange. So, don't refuse to receive what you deserve in exchange for your expertise. With the right mindset, you'll be unstoppable! It will allow you to stay on the right track and meet your goals. Remember that trust and reputation are essential to monetizing your blog. So, don't let opportunities to build trust and reputation slip you by. Become an authority in your niche market and that will earn you their trust and a good reputation.

Remember that writing an eBook is the best way to establish yourself as an authority figure within your niche market. Our minds are trained to associate books with knowledge. So, if you manage to publish on platforms that your ideal readers have access to, like Amazon, your reputation as an authority figure will gradually increase and you'll earn your reader's trust.

I hope you follow every step because it has been a real pleasure to introduce you to them.